Life After Death Beyond Doubt

How my Spirit Guide gave me factual evidence of my previous life on earth

Susan Starkey

Clink Street

London | New York

Published by Clink Street Publishing 2018

Copyright © 2018

First edition.

This is a work of non-fiction. It reflects the author's present recollections of experiences over time. Some names and identifying details have been changed to protect the privacy of individuals.

The author asserts the moral right under the Copyright, Designs and Patents Act 1988 to be identified as the author of this work.

ISBN:
978-1-912262-68-7 - paperback
978-1-912262-69-4 - ebook

DEDICATION

To my wonderful husband for his patience,
understanding and unceasing support.

With special thanks to my Spiritual Teacher and members of The Circle
without whose support, guidance and love this book would not have
been written.

Contents

FOREWORD

I have the greatest of pleasure in introducing this beautiful book, written by Susan Starkey.

I first met Susan when she attended one of my "Circle" group meetings. She arrived with no preconceptions; in fact, she was more inclined to be sceptical and questioned whether a spirit world existed. She didn't understand or know what the spirit world was. She is probably one of the most pragmatic, candid and grounded, yet compassionate women I have ever been privileged to meet. It was apparent to me, when I met her, that Susan was already a natural medium. Little did she know, when she became a member of my Circle, that the spirit world would be communicating through her.

For more than four years Susan attended these meetings, and she has described everything she experienced in this sensitive and thought provoking book.

There are probably thousands of books written on Life After Death. Susan's story I believe is unique - this is a story of a different kind – proving beyond doubt that there is existence beyond the grave. Susan speaks about her discovery of the details of her past life and of her connection with her spiritual guide, who gives her verifiable evidence about his own previous life on earth. She tells of how she found the ability to guide lost souls to the light and pass on to the hereafter.

Susan reveals how she came to understand her life's purpose, which is detailed so eloquently in this book.

I have been a spiritual teacher for over 28 years and in all those years, this is the first time I have witnessed such a life-changing transformation. What Susan has discovered through her automatic writing, and achieved through her contact with her spirit guide, has knocked me sideways.

Most importantly, Susan learned one of the most important lessons of all – how to give love and kindness to all people. I become very emotional and excited when it comes to the spirit world. It is all about love and kindness. Eventually, this message will be spread throughout this world.

In proving there is Life After Death, Susan's aim is to bring comfort and a new understanding to anyone who has concerns or doubts about what happens when they die.

Susan has written about her experiences so movingly and poignantly. I'm thrilled and honoured to introduce her important work, as detailed in this book.

I sincerely hope you will enjoy Susan's inspiring book, as I am so proud of her and what she has achieved.

The Rev. John Bundock
(Known as George in the book)

INTRODUCTION

This is the true story of what happened to me and how I was introduced to the spirit world. It is now my belief that we never truly die.

In recounting the experiences and the messages I received from the spirit world, I sincerely hope that I can help others and provide them with answers to questions they may have about what happens when they die and comforts them with the knowledge I have been given of the great unknown.

This is an account of how I changed from a sceptical, non-believer in life after death to someone who, through the receipt of verifiable evidence from the spirit world, became a true believer that there is indeed life after death.

I was born in the UK. My parents were traditional, middle class English. My father, ironically, was originally destined for the priesthood but cast aside all his beliefs when he married outside the Catholic church, became an atheist and joined the banking industry. His early years of having Catholicism drilled into him turned him into a complete non-believer in God and rigid in his belief that life after death did not exist. My mother, a school teacher, was equally sceptical, although she was a little more flexible in her beliefs and allowed me to attend the local Methodist church, where I was confirmed.

As I grew into adulthood, however, I started to question the purpose of life: was there such a thing as reincarnation and was there a life after death? I tried debating this with my father but I always received the same rigid response, that there was no life after death and that I was talking nonsense.

My life was to follow the same traditional pathway as my parents until I married for the first time. My husband was a diplomat and we lived in a number of developing countries, which subjected me to the impact of different cultures and religious beliefs. I immersed myself in these with a renewed thirst for knowledge.

After my first husband died, I joined the banking industry in the City of London and also became an authority in the British travel industry. I was very down to earth and pragmatic, and at the time I thought I was totally in control of my life and destiny.

However, none of my experiences prepared me for what would transpire in the years to follow.

Little did I know that when I decided to alter my career path and move to Spain, my whole life would be changed for me and unbelievable things would happen to me, quite outside my control. I was to discover that I had had a previous life, and not only that, I discovered my roots and a family that had been lost to me for generations.

If someone had told me this before I left the UK, I would have told them that they lived in cloud cuckoo land. My journey of discovery started in Spain when at the beginning of 2009, two of my friends suggested I accompany them to a spiritualist "Circle" meeting and I did this more to help and humour them, thinking this would be a "one-off".

Nothing in my life's experience had prepared me for what I was to encounter as a result of this meeting; the life changing experiences that were to happen to me as I followed my pathway to "finding the light" and understanding the spirit world.

When I first started writing this book, I talked about it and showed it to a number of friends. Reactions from both my believer and non-believer friends were all the same – they were all incredulous and everyone, without exception, urged me to publish so that my experiences could be read by a much wider audience. In a time of such great uncertainty in the world, my friends thought this book would provide comfort to many others seeking to find the answers that I had been given. One friend even told me that my face lit up and my voice changed when I recounted various messages that I had received.

I sincerely hope that the experiences I have written about in this book about life existing after death, will help all those when their time comes, to have closure in this life and find their way to the next one, in the strong belief that not all ends here and that they have much to look forward to.

* * *

CHAPTER 1

My First "Circle" Meeting

Maybe I was frightened of the future, or concerned that my past would come back to haunt me. Or was it just fear of the unknown? In any event, when I was first asked to join a spiritualist development group, known as "The Circle", I came up with lots of excuses not to go. Fate knew better, and my journey of discovery began!

Little did I know when I joined George and Anne at my first Circle meeting what incredible emotions and discoveries would follow. Not only did I discover my own spirituality and that I was a true medium, but I also found that I had an ability to communicate through automatic writing with the spirit world, through my guardian spirit and guide, Elephally.

Many life-changing experiences were to happen to me as I followed my pathway to "finding the light". This is a true account of events.

When all this started, I had just recovered from a major illness and felt as if my life had returned to near perfection. I had a caring and loving husband whom I adored, a wonderful house in an idyllic setting which I loved, many good friends and a close family. Did I want to spoil any of this perfection with anything new, and what others might perceive to be weird? None of my excuses worked.

Two of my friends knew better. They had both been to the Circle and had returned feeling more at peace with themselves and, more to the point, they were determined that I should go along to the next meeting. So, feeling quite relaxed, and keeping what I thought was an open mind, my husband, Mark, and I arrived at George's house for my first evening participating in the Circle.

George (who was to become my spiritual teacher) is a lovely man and so is his wife Anne; they are both mediums. George spent time explaining to me what the Circle was all about and that there was nothing to fear from it – everything from the spirits, he said, was given with love and kindness. He said that it would be a long slow road to my finding the light and that it would lead to my contacting my guardian spirit and discovering my own spirituality. I found I was becoming quite intrigued by what he was saying about spirit guides – much of what he was saying reminded me of Shirley MacLaine's book, *Out on a Limb*,[1] in which she told of her "out of body" experiences and meeting her spirit guides. I had read this book some 20 years ago and been profoundly affected by it.

Starting with a prayer, and then the opening of our "chakra" points (seven centres of spiritual power in the human body), the nine of us in the Circle were then guided into meditation by George. I had never been able to meditate before, and this was a whole new experience for me. We were asked to envisage a pink mountain with large double doors at the top, leading into a monastery, at which we should knock.

Closing my eyes, I floated up a pink mountain. It was covered in ice and the rays from the sun were turning it pink. I told myself to go more slowly and to take my time floating to the top. When I arrived there, I saw the two large wooden doors and knocked. Nothing happened. Asking myself whether anyone was going to open the door, I knocked again and the door opened. I was conscious that there were people on the other side and it took me a while to work out what I could see. A Buddhist monk, swathed in orange robes, greeted me and led me up a pathway with a wooden hand rail. As I walked up the pathway I could see a black hole, which kept repeating itself, and then a strong silver shining light.

I passed through the black hole and found myself leaving a tunnel, then saw a wonderful green meadow, with a crowd of children playing in it. However, my friendly monk was still drawing me forward, extending his hand to me, this time up a wooded slope, again with a light at the top. At this point, George drew an end to the meditation.

Everyone was then asked to explain what they had seen. I felt quite self-conscious – had I actually meditated or was I just very good at daydreaming? Had I conjured up what I thought I should be seeing?

As I listened to the others' experiences I started to wonder just how George would interpret my meditation. My husband, Mark, who was also new to the Circle that evening and was the first to talk of his meditation, self-consciously said that he had not even reached the monastery doors – he was still walking up the mountain, which according to George indicated that he has a long journey ahead of him. Others in the Circle had incredible visions of colour and altars. Some were much further along the path of understanding their spirituality than others. Then the lady just before me caused memories to surface in my mind that I had long forgotten. She talked of a "pretend" friend.

Now in my early years, from two to five, I had had a pretend friend called "Little Nana", named after my mother's mother, whom I called Nana. My little friend went everywhere with me and on one occasion, when I was out walking with my grandma, we got lost in some woods. So I went behind a tree to pray to Little Nana for help to find our way.

When it came to my turn to recount my meditation, I started by saying that I had had a pretend friend until about the age of five. George said that this was my spiritual guide and that this guide had never left me – I had just stopped talking to him.

With some trepidation, I then recounted my meditation and was totally stunned by George's analysis of it. Probably more to the point, he was also amazed by my meditation at my first Circle meeting. He said that I was a natural medium already and a long way down the path to finding myself and discovering my spirituality, although the ice on the mountain signified that there would be stumbling blocks along the way. The monk, he said, was my guide: the person who had looked after me in my childhood, now making contact with me again and that he would be with me from now on to eternity. My life from now on would never be the same again.

George then asked all of us in the Circle if anyone was receiving any messages. As it was my first time, he asked me to focus on one of the group. Nothing happened. I tried hard to focus on the lady opposite me, but my mind was a blank. Slowly, some of the Circle stood up to pass on messages. One gentleman told me that he saw emeralds and a magician's wand, which didn't make any sense to me. George saw three children looking after me and I tried to think who they might be. He also saw a soldier, dressed in guard duty regalia, complete with the black furry hat that the guards outside Buckingham Palace wear. As this rang no bells, he said that this was another one of my guides, who would help me to overcome my nervousness.

And then it happened. Suddenly, a vision of a Chinese junk in a harbour came to me. It seemed a very odd picture, but nevertheless I took a deep breath and I stood up to say what I had seen. And the lady opposite me said that, yes, it made complete sense to her. George's interpretation was that it was a second chance for this lady and she confirmed that that evening she had received a telephone call offering her exactly that. Wow!

This had been my first experience of the Circle, and I found myself keen to know more. Afterwards, George came up to me to tell me how privileged he felt that I had come to the Circle meeting that evening and that he hoped very much that I would continue to come along to his meetings. If not, he sincerely hoped I would go to other Circle meetings. He explained that I would probably receive a visit from my guide, whom I had called "Ben".

I told George about a visit I had made to a medium when I was in my early twenties. She had told me I was a "young" soul. George said he could quite understand this and that it would become clearer to me in time. I also remembered her telling me that I had been together with a male friend of mine in many previous lives and that we would continue to meet in future lives. She told me that I would live a very materialistic life; that this was my lesson from my current life. She also told me that I still had a great deal of traveling to do, that I would have a wonderful career from which I would gain huge job satisfaction, and that I would meet my second husband in a few years' time. All of this had proven to be correct. I struggled to remember more of what she had told me, but couldn't. I hoped that more might come back to me later.

That evening when I went to bed I was becoming very excited about the possibility of seeing Ben. I again saw a bright light and the image of a monk in the centre, but that was all. The following day, I again saw the light, but this time I saw the full-size image of a monk. Was this Ben, I asked myself? He was a relatively young guy with straight brown hair – not a shaven head – and he was smiling. I also saw the white head of an elderly Chinese Buddha, on a much smaller scale, who kept floating in and out of focus. As I drifted off to sleep I was conscious also of seeing a Roman soldier with a gold metal helmet and gold metal body armour, a shirt, and leather sandals with ties up to the knees. Sadly that was all I saw before I fell into a deep sleep.

I woke up the following morning wondering if all this was for real. Had I been dreaming? Had my imagination been working overtime? Did I really have a spiritual guide who was trying to make contact with me again?

However, over the course of that following week I saw the circle of light many times with the vision of a monk (although I could never clearly see his face), the young lad with the brown hair (whom I decided was different from the monk) and the white head of the Chinese Buddha. I also saw a hand reaching out to me and my own hand joining it, so that two hands clasped together were shown in my vision. Why, I asked, do you not speak to me? I heard a reply saying it was too early; that I had to learn more. Not yet, was the message I was receiving.

I started having recollections of the spirits I had seen in the past. Did these have any bearing on what I was now experiencing? I remember one particular incidence very clearly. I was in my early twenties, staying in a bungalow in the Canary Islands. In fact, on my first arrival on Gran Canaria, when I was nineteen, I had had the distinct feeling that I had been to this island before and that I would continue to visit it many, many times, which proved to be correct.

But that's digressing. Back to the bungalow. It was my last night there and I was woken from a deep sleep to see a man sitting on the bedside table beside me. I was mesmerized by his face, which was deeply scarred and pockmarked. Eventually I managed to tear my eyes away from his face and to turn to my husband. When I turned over again the man had disappeared. I was still talking about this vision in the taxi the following morning on the way to the airport, when the taxi driver interrupted and told me that there had been a fire in the bungalow I had been staying in and that a man had died there. Was this the person I saw?

At other times I have been conscious of bodies being in the same room or walking across a roof terrace – never very clear, just a distinct impression. And then there were the mediums I had visited. Not long after my first husband had sadly died, I visited another medium, wanting to know if it was possible to contact him. Not only did she contact him but she also had a vision of a small blue briefcase, about the size of an A4 piece of paper. Inside this briefcase, she said, was a small computer, which had a secret compartment and which contained the details of a secret overseas bank account. This was quite feasible as my first husband had been an international diplomat working out of Geneva, the home, of course, of secret Swiss Bank accounts.

I rushed home, turned the house upside down, and found the blue briefcase. Sure enough, inside was a small digital diary, which my husband had kept very much to himself. With trepidation, I switched on the diary and found the secret compartment, which I couldn't get into as I didn't have the password. I contacted Casio (the manufacturers of the digital diary), who were extremely helpful and managed to crack the code for me. There were only a few numbers stored and none of them meant anything, although there was one string of numbers that was longer than the rest. I looked up the codes for Swiss bank accounts and discovered that the first digits matched. However, the full string of numbers I had fell between two bank numbers and there was no bank listed for my numbers. To this day I have never been able to find out if there was any money there! And by now it's probably all been used up in charges!

Over the course of about the next ten years I kept in fairly regular contact with this medium, who proved to be incredibly accurate in her predictions, including the fact that I would marry again to a man called Andrew. My second husband was christened Andrew Mark, although he is known as Mark. I also visited a spiritualist in the local church, who passed messages to me from my first husband.

More recently, late one New Year's Eve, I was talking to a friend's son, who from an early age had been receiving messages for people. He told me that there was a very troubled young man who wanted to talk to me, but was making a nuisance of himself so he told him to go away. It was very clear to me that this young man was my second husband's son, who had tragically died in his early twenties – was this one of the three children that George had told me were surrounding me now?

Some of the books I have read – Morris West's *The Clowns of God* [2] and John G. Fuller's *The Ghost of Flight 401* [3] - all had had a profound influence, as they reflected many of my beliefs.

Was this all part of my destiny? Did these ghosts, mediums and books start my path towards learning about my own spirituality? Was I now ready to learn more? The words "you've done well" sprang into my head.

I decided I needed to speak more with George to try and understand my thought process and the visions and memories that I had been experiencing. I wanted to find out about the connection between my mind, body and spirit.

CHAPTER 2

Meeting my Spirit Guides

The following Monday came round very quickly and I had heard nothing more from my spirit guides. Mark rather shyly asked me about what he should expect when he was asked to meditate. I replied that from my own experience, I just let my mind and imagination wander and that he should do the same.

I was actually really looking forward to the meditation session. George asked us this time to imagine going along a country road by whatever form of transport we chose – car, motorbike, bicycle or on foot. The road would lead to a house, and we should explore the garden before knocking on the front door to see what happened next. He said that this evening we were all going to meet our spirit guides.

Finding it much harder this time to let my mind wander, I envisaged myself driving along a country road with open undulating mountain scenery. There was a small dog with me with its paws on the dashboard, looking ahead, and I was talking to it. Eventually we found the track we were supposed to take and arrived at a cottage, with roses growing around the door. This cottage, however, grew in size and I spent time wandering around, seeing a beautifully laid out garden with high stone walls, box hedges, lovely plants and crazy paving pathways – very much a classical country house English garden. There was a small bridge going over a stream leading to a meadow, which I wanted to go into, but I decided it was time to knock on the door.

The door was slowly opened, but I couldn't see who by. I found myself in a large Victorian kitchen with a plump, smiling lady wearing a cloth, frilly hat, and an apron which was covered in flour. However, I was drawn out of the kitchen, again by an unseen person, through French doors onto a terrace where there was a large table around which people were gathered. Again, I couldn't make out any faces except for a blurred vision of an old man. I wasn't allowed to join the group but was guided onto a beautiful lawn with a swimming pool, around which throngs of children were playing. At this point George called everyone back.

Mark was first to recount his meditation. He seemed very overcome by what he had experienced, as he had seen far more than he had in his previous meditation. He had knocked on the door of a house and been guided to a bedroom, where an Indian lady was sitting on the bed under a canopy. She held his hand and together they floated upwards and looked down on the countryside. Mark said that he had the most wonderful feeling of peace and happiness and that he hadn't wanted to be called back.

George was very pleased and surprised by Mark's meditation, saying he had progressed a long way and that the lady he had met was his spirit guide.

Finally it was my turn to recount what I had seen. George told me that the dog I had been talking to was a faithful friend. His spirit guide was telling me that the reason I couldn't see who was showing me around the house was because I was being held back to ensure that I remained pure and didn't develop too quickly. Although I was already a natural medium, my development, he said, would change the person I was, and that this had to be done slowly for me to accept what was happening. I immediately remembered the conversation I had had with Ben earlier that week, when he had said "not yet" to my desire to have a conversation with him.

During our clairvoyance session I was quite disappointed as I didn't really have any visions or messages. Was this lack of vision part of my being held back?

After the Circle closed that evening, I sought out George to try and find an answer to some of the questions buzzing around in my head. I told him about the memories that had come to me about ghosts, books I had read and mediums I had visited and Ben's comment afterwards of "you have done well". George heaved a big sigh of relief and said that this was Ben's blessing to the Circle and that I was in the right place for the time being. He said that at any point Ben might guide me to another Circle. George said that I would be involved in mediumship for a long time, that he was being told that it would not be short-term and asked if I understood this. Goodness, yes.

George was also full of praise for Mark. He said that at our first meeting he was afraid that Mark had joined the Circle only to support me, but after this evening's meeting he now knew this was not the case. He said that Mark was a very special, patient person with a path to follow. I told George that in the past Mark had volunteered with the Samaritans support organisation, which George seemed very pleased to hear.

I felt that I was indeed fortunate to be able to share the "happenings" of our Circle meetings and my feelings with Mark, as we so closely understood each other. It had obviously been Mark's turn that evening to discover more of himself and to meet his guide, and I was delighted for him and excited for myself, even though I had to be a little more patient with my own progress.

Mark and I had joined the Circle late. When we joined it had been the 13th meeting, and according to George the Circle would close to anyone new after the 26th meeting, when the real learning would start. Three months to go, although George explained that it would probably take between two to five years for me to recognize and use my true mediumship. I would be learning about clairvoyance, crystal balls, transient writing and many other things. I would be speaking to large audiences. In fact, he would be arranging for the Circle to meet a psychic surgeon and to help him with his audiences, albeit we would have many practice sessions before this happened.

All this sounded incredible. What had I let myself in for? Did I really believe in all of this? Yes, I did, but with a touch of scepticism. Only time would tell if there really was a journey of enlightenment for me to make.

Three days later, I tried to make contact with a very dear friend, Roger, who was recovering from a perforated stomach ulcer. Despite numerous attempted telephone calls and e-mails I had received no replies and became increasingly concerned. That night I awoke and immediately thought of Roger. I tried hard to concentrate on him to see if I would receive any message. Nothing seemed to happen – and then I saw an image of Jesus Christ with a ring of thorns on his head, and then the words, "don't do anything" came to me. Not really understanding the image, I interpreted the words to mean that I should leave Roger alone. The following day I received an e-mail from Roger saying that he had had a relapse and had been instructed to have complete rest. The words "don't do anything" suddenly had an entirely different meaning – this was obviously a message for Roger, not for me!

Back at the Circle meeting again the following Monday, I could hardly wait for the evening to start, particularly when George said that he was going to throw everyone in the deep end that evening! Great, I said, and George seemed very surprised by my reaction. He started by saying that we should never seek to "limit" ourselves, as this would limit our spirits from helping us.

George produced his crystal ball, which he asked each of us to hold, to feel its weight, to get a sense for it and to then pass it onto the next Circle member. It was my turn first and the crystal ball felt very heavy and very smooth. After we had all taken our turn, George then explained that when he was consulting the crystal ball, he would cover part of it with a cloth to stop the light from clouding its messages. He then asked each of us to envisage a crystal ball in our hands; to then partly cover it with a cloth and to look deep into the crystal ball....

In my mind's eye I could see only a mistiness – the ball was not clear. Slowly, however, I saw a stone terrace with a white balustrade. On the other side of the balustrade was a very blue lake with a mountain in the background. A lady was standing by the balustrade to the left. I tried to concentrate on her to see her more clearly, but my attention was drawn to a young toddler with jet black hair and slanted Chinese eyes. He was playing on a little push scooter and kept looking at me. I was then conscious of him whizzing up a country road, with open space all around and again mountains in the distance. He was laughing and constantly turning round to see me. Suddenly, there were lots of dogs running after him as well.

I was again drawn back to the lady beside the lake, although this time it was dark and I could see the distant lights of a town on the other side of the lake. I then found myself on a boat in front of the town, which turned into a boat that I was rowing up a river in what appeared to be the Amazon jungle. Dense green forest surrounded the river on both sides. Eventually I reached a very green circular pond, and as I rowed into the middle of the lake, the water started to swirl rapidly around until it drained out of the pond. Not knowing what to make of this, I then started to climb up the soil bank.

At this point, George called everyone back from their meditation. I was amazed that I seemed able to meditate. All my endeavours to meditate in the past had proved fruitless – so why was I able to do so now?

I laughingly recounted to the Circle what I had seen in my meditation. George told me that I really was a true medium, that he hadn't in fact expected anyone to see anything in the crystal ball and was truly amazed by all the Circle members' experiences. He then told me that the little boy on the scooter was me and that the scooter signified my path of discovery rushing ahead very quickly. The dogs symbolized all my faithful friends who would accompany me on my journey.

We then went on to a part of the evening that I always seem to find difficult – that of clairvoyance and the receiving of messages. We were asked to imagine that a medium had failed to arrive in front of a gathered audience and that we, individually, had been asked to stand in for the medium and pass on messages.

My message was for Peter. I saw a long narrow track with a hut at the end, which Peter reached. This, I gathered, indicated that Peter was striving to meet a goal and would achieve it.

The gentleman next to me, however, was very clear in his vision of a bowl of yellow chrysanthemums in the middle of the table.

Then an incredible experience happened. George indicated that one of his spirits was coming forward. I watched George's facial expressions change as he went into a semi-trance. It was almost like watching an army sergeant grimace, stand to attention, raise his shoulders upwards and then cross his arms tightly over his body. A voice then started to tell us that there was a Chinese gentleman guide in the middle of the table, who was there to help us. This gentleman was very powerful and we should contact him with our questions and needs.

After George came out of his trance he said that the yellow chrysanthemums represented the golden light and that this was the Chinese gentleman guide.

I continued to attend the Circle meetings. The meditation sessions I found relatively easy but try as hard as I could, I couldn't receive any clairvoyant messages. This led me to question whether my meditations were just my overactive imagination, and as nothing particularly remarkable happened for a number of meetings, this also made me question whether I really was a natural medium.

Then George, our teacher, had to go away for a few weeks and Anne, his wife and also a medium took over. She was determined to speed up our progression before George returned and the Circle meetings took on a different format. They became more informal with a great deal of laughter and she spent time answering our questions. Mark was particularly keen to understand why he needed to meditate. She told him that basically, meditation helped to clear his mind to enable his spirit guides and helpers to make contact with him. She said that everyone was capable of becoming a medium and receiving messages from their guides; some people just took longer than others.

On this particular evening, however, we didn't start with our usual meditation. Anne asked each of us in turn to stand up, choose one of the group, and to say the first thing that came to mind, whether this be a vision, a voice saying something or a feeling.

I wasn't looking forward to my turn as I didn't think I would manage to get any messages. However, I kept my mind purposely blank. I was the last person to stand up and I chose Jessica. I tried to hear messages, but as before heard nothing. However, I became very conscious that my hands had covered my face – something I would never normally do. So I asked Jessica if she was hiding from something or didn't want to face up to something. The palms of my hands then opened up and one hand covered the other, leading me to question whether she wanted to open up about something or uncover something, and that the timing was now right to do so. Anne asked Jessica if she knew anyone who used their hands to gesture and she said that her mother had when she was alive. She said she could also accept my suggestion that there was something she didn't want to face up to and that she would now tackle this. She gave me 9.5 out of 10, so I must have got something right.

It did restore my faith in my ability to progress and I again started to look forward to our weekly Circle meetings.

CHAPTER 3

Contact from the Spirit World

Mark and I continued to go to Circle meetings but neither of us felt that we were really achieving anything and I continued to find it difficult to be "clairvoyant". We did however invite George and Anne to our house for lunch one day, which was very enjoyable and inevitably the conversation turned to the Circle. Mark continued to question what it was all about and if he would ever become a medium. Then, completely out of the blue, George said to Mark that he had a young man on the spirit side who wanted to make contact and would continue to do so. I knew immediately who this young man was, and disappeared into the kitchen as I was feeling very emotional. I returned to find Mark rushing out of the dining room in tears, with George hot on his trail. When they returned, Mark was still crying but they were tears of happiness. George had told him that it was his "boy" and that the message was that he was very happy in his spirit life. There was no way that George could have known that Mark had a son who had died in his early twenties and so we both edged a little further along our path of believing in the spirit world.

The following Monday's Circle meeting dawned and we were both looking forward to the meeting. We again started with a five minute meditation, when we were asked to imagine a church, to go through the door of the church and walk to a lectern to find a book and to then see what the book had to say. My five minute meditation passed very quickly; in fact it didn't seem possible that five minutes had passed. I had found my church and walked up a path through a graveyard, where there was a cherubic blond curly-haired angel with wings floating above me and drawing me forward. As I entered the church I was greeted by a priest with a purple shoulder cover. He gestured for me to continue up the aisle, past a congregation, until I reached the lectern. I climbed the steps and looked at a bible, but saw nothing. I asked my guiding spirit to help me and was then drawn through the book so that I was floating upwards on the end of a bell cord with bells ringing and I could see the sun coming through the tops of trees. I looked down at the priest, who told me to continue upwards, which I did until I passed above the trees and continued towards a bright light.

In interpreting this, George said that this was my journey with my guides helping me forward.

All the other Circle members also had meditations that were meaningful. I felt as if we had all somehow moved up a step in our understanding and that we were learning to clear our minds to be receptive to messages from the spirit world.

George then asked us to look at one of our fellow Circle members and to see who, from the spirit world, was standing beside them. George said he saw a monk beside me who would be making contact regularly over the next six months. I immediately recollected the Buddhist monk I had encountered in my first meditation, whom I believed to be my childhood pretend friend. I looked at one of my fellow Circle members and also saw a monk standing beside her, with a brown habit with the hood shading his face and a rope tied around his waist. This was the first time I had seen a vision, and so for the first time since I had started with the Circle, I truly believed that I was achieving something and would continue to progress.

Unfortunately, the weather took a turn for the worse which made it impossible to attempt the long drive to George and Anne's for the next couple of Circle meetings, so we effectively missed two meetings.

The car drive, when we did eventually make a meeting, was a nerve-wracking drive through torrential rain, with large boulders rolling down the mountainside all around us. When we reached George and Anne's we found that only Mark, myself and Veronica had managed to get there.

Right from the start, this evening felt different. It was much more relaxed, with light-hearted banter before we started our meditations. We were asked to imagine ourselves riding a bike with green fields on the left hand side and cottages on the right. We were to knock on the door of the cottage which seemed to be attracting us. George explained that the recounting of our meditations allowed him to see how far each of us was progressing.

Mark and Veronica both saw their spirit guides in their meditations. My meditation, however, was different from those I had received before. I rode my bike down a slope, passing the green fields on the left, and occasionally saw a cottage on the right but none attracted me to the front door. I asked Ben, my guide, to help me and started riding uphill. At this point I was aware of a cottage which I couldn't see clearly. As I knocked, the door was flung open and I was swept up into an orange fireball, which took me up out of the cottage, through snow-clad fields, where Ben said it was all alright, and I continued up into a night sky with countless stars; then in the distance I saw a vision of Christ with his long brown hair and a white robe. He beckoned me forward and told me I could slow down now and that he was going to introduce me to my guides. The first was a Turkish belly dancer; then came my Roman soldier, then my Japanese lady, and then a young lad with a little puppy.

George was over the moon when I recounted my meditation, saying that this was what everyone should be striving for. I had progressed to another dimension and the rapidity of my understanding of the spirit world would help my fellow Circle members to progress quicker.

We were then asked to pass on messages to members of the Circle. I saw George with a white circular glow around his head, standing in an archway, which became a double door into a church and either he or another man was standing at the top of steps by this door with a young bride at their side. George said he could completely understand this message.

This evening had been the first time that I really felt as if I could receive clairvoyant messages and it felt incredible.

CHAPTER 4

Learning about Clairvoyance and Mediumship

The next couple of meetings, to my mind, were uneventful. The only significant part of one of my meditations was seeing my Roman soldier guide who told me we had "wars to wage".

Then another breakthrough occurred.

We were asked to imagine a flower of our choice; to look at this flower and to see what followed. I envisaged a yellow chrysanthemum (my favourite flower) but this was rapidly replaced by a field of sunflowers, swinging gently in the breeze against a clear blue sky. Coincidentally, several of my fellow Circle members also saw sunflowers in their meditations, but with a different emphasis. For me, the central brown part of the flower became a smiling face and the eye winked at me. Then I saw my Roman soldier again, on horseback with his army behind him. He told me to stop wasting time with flowers and to get on my horse, which I did. We galloped towards a drawbridge and fortification. There was a much smaller horse with a small man in chain armour, who fell off or was pushed off his horse, but he immediately climbed back on it again.

27

I followed my soldier into a banqueting hall, where I asked him what the significance of my flower was. He told me that this meant "health" as far as I was concerned. (This was very significant for me and very reassuring after all my health problems). He also told me we were in the banqueting hall to enjoy ourselves and that we were being joined by the man who had fallen off his horse, who in fact was the court jester, who had come along to show that we shouldn't take things too seriously and that we should enjoy ourselves. I was then conscious of being on horseback again, riding with my soldier and his army. At this point the meditation ended.

George told me that a yellow chrysanthemum signified a Chinese guide and that this guide had shown me the field of sunflowers. George was particularly pleased that I had seen an army, as this meant that all these spirits were present to help me and the Circle. He said that I would probably have a large number of guides presenting themselves to me. The message I had received about enjoyment and laughter was also very pertinent.

We then moved on to concentrate on clairvoyance. I was asked to concentrate on Peter. I always found clairvoyance difficult, so I looked at Peter's eyes, which were a clear blue, and I could see water, either sea or a lake, with Peter standing on the shoreline looking out wondering what to do. This apparently was very pertinent, as Peter used to be a keen sailor and wanted to re-start this pastime. I also saw a wooden door which was partly open. This, George said, signified Peter's entry into the spirit world.

Jessica then stood up and told me she had a lady called Betty wanting to contact me. This lady, she said, would have been in her prime years in the 1930's/1940's. She had dark shoulder-length hair and had lived in the south of England. Her message to me was to enjoy my mediumship and to continue being "Roman".

I was thrown by this message. My previous late husband's mother had been called Betty; she had dark shoulder-length hair and, yes, she would have been in her prime as she had given birth in 1942 in London and had originally hailed from South Wales. The fact that Betty was trying to contact me made me feel very warm and happy.

At this point, George decided to put a silver casting of the head of a Roman soldier on the table as he hoped this would stimulate my clairvoyance. I heard this soldier saying he wanted to talk to me, and that I should tell George how much he appreciated being put on the table and that he would be present at many more future meetings. George seemed particularly pleased with this message, although I still had my misgivings that my imagination might have put those words into my head.

I then saw my Roman soldier again, galloping forward with his army with an orange flag flying behind him as he surged forward. Progress? Time will tell. George keeps telling us that our group is progressing very quickly as our help is needed in the world. It will be interesting to look back in a year's time to see our growth. Apparently, on the outside of our Circle is another Circle of spirits who are there to learn from us. They are silent at the moment, but as they learn more they may well make an input.

I pondered on how many more guides I would find that I had. So far, I have my Buddhist monk (Ben), my Roman soldier, my Japanese lady, my two Chinese guides, a Turkish belly dancer and a young boy, a table full of faceless diners and a Roman army! Quite exciting.

Unfortunately, after this I missed seven weeks of Circle meetings due to snow and also a rather long holiday in India. I was a little surprised that none of my guides sought to make contact with me during this period, but apparently they too like a holiday to recharge their batteries.

It was a full Circle meeting of the seven remaining members when I eventually sat down with them on a bright sunlit afternoon to meet my next challenge. George explained that he would like all of us to imagine that we were going into a hall for a clairvoyant evening. We should buy a ticket at the entrance, sit down in the audience and then discover that because the medium had not turned up that we would be asked to go up on stage and give readings. After the meditation he wanted us to pretend we were still on the stage and to give each other messages/readings.

So I entered my meditation and found that all seven of us were sitting in a row together. There was a fuss on stage about the medium not turning up and George turned to me and told me that I should go up on the stage and take over. I climbed up a staircase onto the stage and introduced myself, saying that this was the first time I had tried to pass messages to people in an audience and that I didn't know whether or not I would be able to but that I would try. I asked my guides for help, but nothing really seemed to be happening. Then I had a message for a friend of mine from her father, there followed a message for a little boy in the audience, and finally I had a vision of a large clock and at this point we were called out of our meditations by George.

Four other members of the Circle gave their readings before me and passed on messages that were meaningful. When it came to my turn I stood up in some trepidation as I truly felt that because I hadn't really received any messages during my meditation it would be unlikely that I would receive any now. But George encouraged me to just say whatever came into my mind.

First of all I saw wide open countryside conveying a sense of peace and tranquillity for Jenny. Then I saw cherries with a feeling of the dark deep colour red of the cherries for Peter. For Jessica I saw a little boy scrabbling around in the dust, and for Mark I saw an old-fashioned sweet shop with jars of different sweets on show. Then again I saw a clock.

George was ecstatic. My reading was apparently totally different from the messages the others had passed on. He said my reading was true mediumship and that I had jumped from clairvoyance to this. He had also had a message from the spirit guides that they were taking over and didn't need any help from him. He said that I would have a difficult few weeks before things became even clearer. Jenny accepted my vision of the countryside as the only real time she had been tranquil was as a child in the country. Peter said the previous day he had been talking about making cherry jam (hence the colour). Jessica had had the little boy referred to by others in the Circle, and Mark confirmed that he liked old-fashioned things. My vision of the clock apparently signified time being called by my guides, which George said would be part of all my future visions. Stunned, I sat down.

So that concluded the Circle meeting. We had all been able to pass on messages to each other and this seemed to signify a big turning point for us all.

CHAPTER 5

My First Sighting of Elephally

This did seem to have been a big turning point. At our next meeting George asked us to tune into our vibrations by putting our hands below our knees to see what we felt, and gradually raising our arms to the top of our heads.

I felt warmth as I rested my hands below my knees and when my hands got to the top of my head I felt as if something was pushing upwards.

After this George encouraged us to have an out of body experience in our meditation. I was conscious of sitting on a wooden chair in the Circle and having a feeling of rising up and seeing a golden cherub high above me. I saw myself as a red amoeba looking down and I was encouraged to look down further through blue skies and a blue lake; then I saw my body rising upwards towards a wonderful golden angel. When I recounted my vision afterwards I found myself bursting into tears when I described rising upwards towards the golden angel. I was surprised by just how emotional I was.

Between this and the following Circle meeting, I met by chance two of George's colleagues. The first was a psychic surgeon and the second a clairaudient. George was delighted to be able to introduce both of these people to me.

At our following meeting George gave us a choice of meditation scenarios, one of which included a conversation with one of our guides. I chose the one that involved exploring an old Roman village leading towards a bridge. I was quite surprised, when wandering around the Roman village, when I met my Roman soldier guide, whom I have now named "Nero", and he stopped me to talk to me. I found myself saying to him that he was obviously changing my meditation so that we could have a conversation, but that I didn't know what to say to him. (George later told me that this was good because I was talking to my guide as a fellow being and not putting him on a pedestal). Nero told me that I should stop trying to talk and to listen, feel and focus more clearly on the things around me. For example, he said I should see colours more vividly (I then saw a bright red poppy in a field). I then saw Nero's army to one side in the Roman village and I focused again on Nero's face. His head was covered in a chain mail helmet and his face was suntanned and strong. I then saw another of my guides, the rotund lady with a white cloth frilly hat, an apron, and hands covered in flour. At this point we were called back.

All the others in the Circle had managed to have out of body experiences to different degrees, and George was absolutely delighted and, I think, a little surprised.

We then turned our attention to the clairvoyant part of the meeting. I saw a man with his head covered in a hood between Jenny and Peter. He then removed his hood and I could see him sitting leaning onto a walking stick for support. He had shoulder-length silver/grey wavy hair which had a central parting. I wasn't sure here whether it was a message for Jenny or Peter but George intervened to say that this was not the case. The person I was seeing was the gathered spirits teacher. He was amazed that I had been able to see him.

I later learned that this vision was highly significant, and that this spirit teacher would play a very important part in my life.

When it was my turn to stand up and give messages to the Circle, I found I was beginning to enjoy myself and that, if I let myself relax, images came immediately to mind. I saw a wooden box being opened by Jenny, signifying the start of something new. For Mark, I saw a rooftop view of church domes on the skyline; for Peter I saw the colour orange and then a sunset with blue sky below the orange, signifying that he too would be starting a new venture. For Anne, I saw a baby with a white bonnet, and for George I saw a wardrobe. Amazingly, everyone could see meanings attached to these messages.

I have to backtrack a little at this stage, because Peter had read my tarot cards for me the previous Sunday. When I had told George that I was very impressed with his reading he asked me if Peter had asked any questions during the reading and when I said no, he was delighted as he felt that Peter had reached his own turning point.

My tarot reading was amazingly accurate. Peter had started by saying that I felt a need to constantly prove myself, even though I knew that I was good at what I did, but was always striving to do better. He said that I needed to relax more and admit when I wasn't quite perfect and if I did this then other things/occupations would enter my life. He saw me juggling many different projects and that it was time to get rid of clutter in my life. He saw a man in his 60's who had a short fuse, who was there to help me (this described my husband). He also saw a young fair-haired boy who I would have much in common with, and also a man in his 40's who was extremely successful and whose advice I should value. He said this man would give advice only when asked and that he would put it in such a way that left room for me to come to my own conclusions. My mind immediately focused on my young nephew and my brother. (The advice that my brother did indeed give me in later life was always given only when asked for). The rest of the reading basically reiterated that I should make way for new things to come into my life.

At the end of the Circle meeting, George congratulated all of us. He said we had achieved in just under a year what previous Circles had taken three or four years to achieve. He said he expected all of us in the next eighteen months to be able to stand on stage and give readings.

CHAPTER 6

Readings to Complete Strangers

Well, we were all in for a complete and stunning surprise at our next meeting. As usual, we gathered at George's, who told us that we were now entering what was effectively Chapter 2 of our Circle learning, something that would normally take four years to achieve. He said that he never promised anything, but that today he would promise big surprises for us all. He said that we now had to learn to trust our spirit guides and that our meditation this time was to focus on one of our guides and listen to their message for the Circle.

At the start of the Circle meeting, Mark had been a little concerned because there was an empty chair in our Circle, but both he and Jenny saw a Native American sitting there. All was revealed, however, when Anne left the room to bring in two strangers. George explained that we were all to give these two people a reading and asked for a volunteer to start. I decided that it was better to get it over with and so stood up.

I saw a key and a lock which I interpreted as the Circle unlocking my clairvoyance. I turned to the lady newcomer and said that I saw a pair of scissors and asked whether she was thinking about cutting her hair or had recently been asked to cut someone else's. I also saw a white lit candle. Anne, who was sitting next to the lady, said that she could accept both. I then saw a dusty track leading up into the mountains, with an old broken-down building at the end of the track. I saw this being renovated, and also saw that it would be wonderful when finished. I also saw a clear blue sky with birds flying overhead. I later learned that one of the strangers, for whom I was giving this reading, was renovating an old house in an area many miles to the north of us and that there they had migrating birds.

Mark stood next. He saw an old grey Hillman Imp car, which the male visitor confirmed had been his first car. He also saw an old-fashioned kitchen with a large cooking range and lots of wicker baskets and herbs hanging from the ceiling. The lady confirmed that Mark was totally correct about her kitchen.

Jenny however was the star of the "show". Her reading was far more spiritual, and she focused on the inner turmoil that the lady was feeling in trying to adapt to her new lifestyle. Jenny was so correct that the lady burst into tears.

At the end of our readings we were all given marks out of 10 for accuracy. No-one had anything less than a 9. The couple said that they had been bowled over by our accuracy. However, I still felt that I had a long way to go. It was one thing to see a book or a key; it is quite another to give that vision meaning, the way Jenny had done with her reading.

George, however, was delighted with us all and we all felt pretty proud of ourselves. Later that evening, talking to Mark, he turned to me and said that there must be something in this. How else could he have seen so accurately the colour and type of car? I felt that this was Mark's turning point. He had ceased being a sceptic and was learning to trust what he saw and the messages he was receiving.

At our next meeting George couldn't stop talking about how our two "guinea pigs" the previous week had been bowled over by the accuracy of our readings. They had apparently continued well into the evening talking about just how amazing it had been and how remarkable it was that we were beginners.

George then felt the need to explain further some of the issues we had raised at the previous meeting, particularly how we should interpret symbols. He said we should ask the person whom the message was for if the particular symbol meant anything and if not to then give the meaning of the symbol. For example, a snake and a coffin would mean someone who couldn't be trusted and the loss of something, and the message there would be that for a lady she should watch her jewellery and personal possessions and for a man that he should watch his wallet.

To put everything into context, we should see ourselves as children with a picture book. First of all a child sees a picture, then they learn to read, and then they learn to interpret. This was pretty much the same for us.

He said that we had to learn to trust our spirit guides and that slowly our clairvoyance would turn from earthly visions to spiritual messages.

At this point I again saw the old grey-haired man leaning on his walking stick on the outside of the Circle. This was the spirits teacher whom I had seen before. He was calling all the spirits to gather round to listen and learn from what George was saying and also learn from our questions and feedback. I could feel the spirits pressing around behind me and I also saw Ben, my Buddhist monk, sitting smiling beside a calm blue lake, meaning that everything was calm around us. I passed my vision on to the Circle, and others then said that they too had received messages and seen visions.

I felt that our questions marked a big change for all of us. We had somehow taken control of the meeting, so that what was happening was out of George's control. We had moved on to another level, inspired by the previous weeks' readings, totally believing in our abilities and wanting to learn more.

CHAPTER 7

Experiencing Psychometry and Time Standing Still

Apparently our "guinea pigs" were still talking incredulously about our reading! Our next meeting turned out to be another interesting and giant step forward for us all. George talked about raising our vibrations and gave us a meditation so that he could see how far we had progressed. We were asked to visualize a flower with a defined colour and to see what happened.

I visualized a yellow chrysanthemum (yellow signifying I was on the right path) and I saw my golden cherub angel sitting on the side of the flower. The flower then changed to show the face of a man, and my white-headed Buddha appeared. I then saw hands cupped upwards around the flower and a crystal ball emerging which floated upwards, with the figure of a man trying to reach for it, but his hands were tied behind his back. Slowly, his hands became free and he swam into the crystal ball which continued rising upwards above the skyline. The man then called for me to join him, which I did, and I asked him what the purpose was of my being there. The man told me to look down. Doing this I saw the Arizona desert with my Roman soldier riding fast through a mountainous gulley, followed by chariots and his soldiers. I then saw a dirt track leading upwards through the fields and then a chapel full of monks with one holding onto the bell pulley and floating upwards.

I asked what all this meant and was told that I was now free to hear, feel and see the messages that I would receive; that I should now return back to my flower and at this point George called us back.

All of us had had similar meditations where we rose upwards and saw our guides. Some of us saw yellow flowers, others purple flowers, meaning that they would become healers.

George had asked all of us to bring with us an item close to us which could be held hidden in a hand. He then produced a tray with these items on it hidden under a cloth. We were each asked to pick out an item, to feel the item and then to give a reading. It was important that we didn't know who the item belonged to.

I received a ring, and on turning it over in my hand I saw a large expanse of water and a boat going to my right. I then saw a wooden hut with long grass around it and a bonfire with people gathered around it partying, but reading books at the same time and then dancing. I received the message that this person would be going on a long journey and that it would be the right decision.

I was knocked sideways when the person I gave the reading to later told me that the ring had been a present from her husband whilst they were in Bali (so a long way over water), that they had been staying in a very basic area and that it had been a time of great joy.

All of us were able to give readings which were accurate and meant something to the receiver. This was called "Psychometry", which apparently is widely used by mediums around the world when they give readings.

Then another astounding experience happened. Driving to the next Circle meeting we came across a very nasty car accident which had just happened. Going around a bend, we saw a car, completely wrecked and upside down on the road, with a man underneath it. The accident had obviously just happened. We immediately telephoned the emergency services and went to help the injured man, who amazingly was crawling out of the wreckage. He was badly injured and we tried to console him whilst waiting for the ambulance. When the ambulance arrived, we then travelled on to the Circle meeting.

We had been at the scene of the accident for at least thirty minutes, but incredibly we were not late arriving at George's. Somehow, time had stood still whilst we were helping the injured man. Was this another demonstration of the spirits' intervention? Was it destiny that had brought us to the spot of the accident to help this man, and had the spirits stopped time so that we could still arrive at the Circle meeting on time?

CHAPTER 8

Experiencing Automatic Writing

A few more meetings passed and I seemed to almost stagnate and found it difficult getting messages. So I was delighted when we turned our attention to automatic writing, which was to mark a major turning point in my life.

We were all given paper and pencils and asked to put the point of the pencil on the paper and wait to see what happened. Almost immediately I found my hand moving the pencil in a line across the page and then down, along and back up forming a box. I wrote down:

"In this box you will find a castle. This is your symbol. There will be a new direction in your path. Keep focused, keep your mind within this box."

I then waited and my hand moved of its own volition and I found myself writing in a completely different style of handwriting from my own and it remained consistent in its style. The writing itself made no sense, although one word "*elephally*" kept repeating itself, albeit spelt differently each time, and then the words at the end read *"do what you feel is right."*

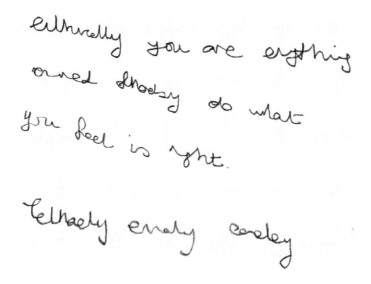

George told me that a famous automatic writer, Matthew Manning [4], had started in this way with writing that was indecipherable at the start, but from there developed his ability to write automatically. I will read his books. Peter also told me about Neale Donald Walsch, who wrote *Conversations with God* [5] – another book to read.

This was my first inkling that this might be my pathway and that I would become an automatic writer.

The others in the Circle all wrote messages or drew pictures.

Mark said he felt as if he had written a tablet of commandments. His automatic reading read, "All forms of being are equal so do not separate them. Everything has a life and it is precious. Time is a great healer: do not run through life, walk. It is for you to make decisions not someone else. I want you to try harder. You must approach with an open heart. You will reap what you sow, be careful what you plant. George, trust your instinct it will be right. Leave the doubters."

Peter drew a picture of a man and a ruin on a mountainside with a moon to the left. It was very clear to us all that the picture was of a man from the Inca time and that the building was his settlement. Was this Peter's guide showing himself?

George drew two feathers with a signature from "two rivers", one of his spirit guides.

We were all pleased with ourselves and our achievements that night and asked that we could repeat this exercise in a couple of weeks.

I didn't have to wait two weeks for my next experience of automatic writing. The following day, whilst writing about my experiences and feelings from the previous evening's Circle meeting, I felt the urge to see if I could write any more.

I put my pen to paper and asked the spirits if they wanted to write anything. Again I felt my hand being guided across a piece of paper and I started writing (with my eyes closed) in a handwriting that was not my own. It started off indecipherably again, although the second word was either

"healing" or "helping" in a (unintelligible word) Lucy."

It went on to read:

"typically in your heart you will (unintelligible word) be drawn to this. .... Chosen ... everything written. Yes this is for Mark. This is a warning. This is a warning to watch his back and be careful of fire. Everything will be OK but you must watch out. Jack must go to hospital he needs treatment quickly. You must help him. Don't delay. You are his friend. You will find this becomes easier, you will need to practice and then you will be able to help others. Call Jack now and tell George not to worry his son will have his operation. We are looking after him, helping, everything ... else, everything will be (eventually?) esovled. Keep doing this to learn."

I immediately called my friend Jack, to find that he was already at the hospital waiting to be admitted later that afternoon. He was not well, and his scan results had shown that the abscess on his liver had grown larger again. I tried to impress on Pat, his wife, that he must be checked into the hospital today, and fortunately he was.

I also telephoned George to tell him about the results of my automatic writing and he was absolutely delighted. He said the message for Mark was warning him of a false friend whom he should be careful of. He said my telephone call to tell him of my work made all his work in helping all of us in the Circle worthwhile.

Unfortunately, George and Anne had to return to the UK and so there were no Circle meetings for four weeks. However, during this break I continued with my automatic writing. Certain indecipherable words kept repeating themselves, particularly the word "*elypally*". I was told to go to this "*elypally*". My guide wrote:

"*I am saying you must go to another, each one will be in "layden", written in another place. You must be careful and let others speak to you. For Jack, he is going to have another operation. You must help him. He wants Pat. Either go or call, hot but will cool. Time will help. Keep trying and you will be drawn to help others. Be at peace with yourself. Do not rush. Keep trying, eventually you will succeed. This is your journey and you will travel down this road.*"

And then I had another breakthrough. I had another written message where my hand seemed to glide across the paper of its own accord. The written message basically said:

"*You will listen to me "elypally". Important within. Listen to what you hear. I am elypally, I am your guide and I will help you to see and hear. Listen to me. Just be yourself and you will be placed in vision in what you do. I will be there and so will others to help you to see where you are going. Eye think you must listen to what we are saying to you. You will understand and you will learn. Listen to yourself.*"

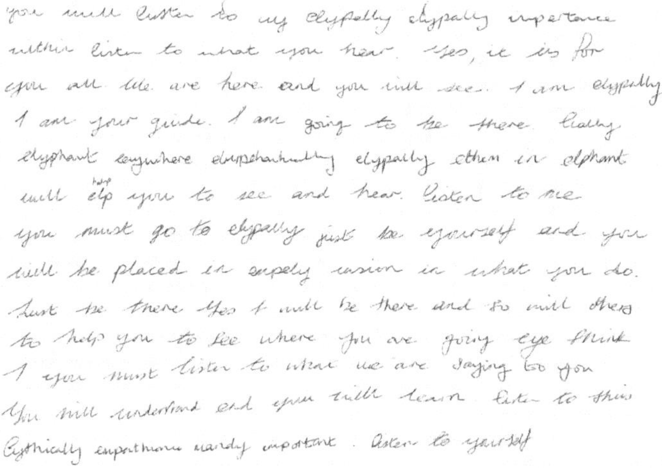
you will listen to my elypally elypally importance
within listen to what you hear. Yes, it is for
you all. We are here and you will see. I am elypally
I am your guide. I am going to be there. Really
elyphant everywhere [illegible] elypally othem in elphant
will help you to see and hear. Listen to me
you must go to elypally just be yourself and you
will be placed in [illegible] vision in what you do.
Just be there. Yes I will be there and so will others
to help you to see where you are going eye think
I you must listen to what we are saying to you
You will understand and you will learn. Listen to this
Eythically [illegible] [illegible] important. Listen to yourself

Finally, George and Anne returned from the UK and we all gathered for another Circle meeting. I showed George copies of my automatic writing, as I was keen to know if this was just my imagination again, or whether I had a real talent for this form of mediumship. George confirmed that this was so.

I was particularly concerned about the message I had received for Jack and I wanted to know what the right way would be to pass on this message. George said that I would be guided, and strangely I had been. I had been researching on the internet looking for liver specialists in the UK and had written the name of two hospitals on a piece of paper, which I had given to Pat, his wife. George said I could only pass on messages and it was then up to the individual who received the message to act on it in their own way.

Our meditation that evening was to walk along a beach, feeling the sand, and to sit down and to see what happened. When I sat down I looked to the left and saw Ben, my monk guide, running along the sand towards me and I looked to the right and saw Nero, my Roman soldier guide. They both took me upwards, floating towards a bright light. I asked them what

I was supposed to be learning from this and they told me to continue to listen.

Next George gave us all a piece of paper, face-down so that we could not see the name written on it. He asked us to hold the paper in our hands and to pass on messages. I immediately heard the name Peter and saw a face with a trembling lip and received the message not to be sad. I was then told that this person should look forward to Christmas and the snow and that they were waiting for a telephone call and should continue taking their medicine. I then turned over my piece of paper to see Anne's name written on it. She gave me 3 out of 3 for accuracy. What was so incredible was that the person she was worried about is called Peter and that she had just received a reassuring telephone call. Only the previous day she had been talking about Christmas and her yearning to see snow. It was also true about her needing to continue to take medicine for her health.

George's message to me that night was that he saw a book being written, which was later to be proved correct.

At our next Circle meeting, George also spent a lot of time talking about our progression that day into Stage 3, another turning point for us all. He said our paths were becoming more clearly defined. Mine was going to be through my automatic writing; Jessica's through the use of a pendulum; Jenny through her natural clairvoyance; Peter possibly through his automatic drawing and Mark, well we had to wait to see what path he chose. George said it was now time for us to start giving clearer messages and to focus more on what we felt. Anne's spirit guide likened it to our having passed through infant school and now starting junior school.

George continued to talk about mediums and clairvoyants who charge excessively for their work, which he clearly felt was not right. He was very upset by "end of the pier" mediums whom he felt were abusing their gifts. This, he felt, was not the true way of spreading love and light. We, he said, were being trained to become pure mediums to help the world, in which we are so desperately needed.

We progressed to talking about books that had been written on the subject, and here George had a completely different view. Books, he said, were there to enlighten and teach others and a payment was for the author, for the time they had spent learning about the spirit world. I didn't mention to George that I had started writing this book, but I felt as if some sort of blessing was being given.

Whilst George was talking I was conscious of a monk in a brown habit standing behind George, whispering in his ear and then dancing and lifting his bare feet into the air. At this point the monk ran away up a dirt track, smiling and waving. George said this monk had been around him all day and that his dancing clearly meant that he was pleased with what we were doing. George seemed delighted that I had seen this monk too.

We then went on to give each other messages. Jessica turned to me and said she saw a Japanese lady, at which point Jenny exclaimed that she had seen this lady too, leading me down a drawbridge onto a boat where there were other Japanese ladies holding umbrellas for me to sit under. Jenny described the first Japanese lady as having a parasol, wearing a traditional Japanese dress, with a white painted face. This was an accurate description of my Japanese spirit guide as I had seen her previously, welcoming me as part of the spirit world.

At the end of the Circle meeting, I told everyone present that I had again tried my hand at automatic writing earlier that afternoon. My writing had become clearer with many more readable words, and again the name "Elypally" was present. As before, my message started with gobbledygook, but rapidly took on meaning. It read:

"Liquid typically e think in light .... Writing elypally. Each one will be found. Shape elypally will be elypally. Happen when you go there. Jack isn't good. He must go to them. They are good. They will help him. Yes it is written, it isn't what you think. You must go. There is a blackboard with a picture of the sea and the sun and Jack is smiling. Anne must smile too. She has great strength. Listen to what you hear and you will be able to help. Lots of water around

and birds in the sky. You must look and listen. Wait eye think you will go to, eye think you must go to help Jack. Yes your guides are here and they will speak to you. You must be patient, the time will come for you to do our work. Listen carefully and learn. We are with you. Keep trying."

I was beginning to feel a little embarrassed by what the others saw as a major step forward on my part, and interestingly that they all seemed to take heart that things were being achieved by the Circle. It was obvious that we were all learning from each other.

George, however, advised me to tread very carefully with any message that I passed on to Jack and that maybe at the present time it would be better just to be there to support him, as it was not clear on which "side" the spirits would be helping him.

However I was delighted to learn the next day that Pat, Jack's wife, had taken the contact name and number of a hospital in London I had given her and had called them for a second opinion. She had been able to speak to a consultant who said that Jack's condition had probably been caused by drinking the water from the local fresh water lakes and that the hospital he was in were doing exactly what he would be doing if Jack were in his hospital. It would take a long time for Jack to recover, but everything was being done correctly. This had obviously given some comfort to Pat and I was delighted for her. Suddenly, however, I was stunned to realize that in my automatic writing of the previous day there had been reference to "lots of water and birds in the sky" – this was where Jack had been drinking the infected water which had given him an amoeba infection.

I called George to pass on this latest revelation, which he said gave him a tremendous uplift as well, at a time when he too needed it. I promised myself I would try automatic writing again during the course of the next week. I was beginning to feel as if I was really achieving something and it gave me a lovely warm feeling in my heart, even though I was still incredulous at what was happening.

CHAPTER 9

Elephally and his Messages

At the next Circle meeting, we all tried our hands again at automatic writing. Having been successful previously, I was somewhat nervous as to whether I would continue to receive any messages. All the others started writing frantically and I waited for my hand to start writing. Very slowly, I managed to write half a page, which read:

"Elypally is here. Wait and listen, ensure that everything is locked. Look towards the horizon and see the light. Elypally will be there. Look and listen to the birds. Flow in time. Enjoy yourself. Eventually there will be light. Keep looking at the mountains, they are significant as this is where you will find what you are looking for. Jewels and sunshine will radiate. Look towards the east where the birds are. Neighbours will help. They will walk towards you. When you are ready you will find elephant. Elapse in everything, even in darkness, especially in autumn."

ekpally is here. Want and listen ..... that everything is looked will towards the horizon and see the light. Elypally will be there will and listen to the birds. Slow in time enjoy yourself eventually there will be light keep looking at the mountains they are significant as this is where you will find what you are looking for Lords and Sunshine will radiate here towards the east where the birds are. Neighbours will help they will walk towards you When you are ready you will find depart Elapse in everything. even in darkness especially in autumn.

An elephant apparently signifies "big things" and birds signify "freedom".

Mark's writing was also very interesting:

"Can you hear me. I would like to help you and it is quite difficult but we will run at the end. How do you feel. Just let your mind go blank and we will pass information to you. Tell everyone they are all doing very well, it is good to watch you all working so hard. Try and relax and it will be easier for you. Down by the river there are many things to see, some are hidden, you will not learn everything at once – it takes time. You must open your mind to what we have to say. Can you hear us? It will get louder in time. Think about the one in the light. You can choose the path to enlightenment. It is time to go."

And then Mark had drawn a symbol of a diamond which signifies work in many ways.

Before the following Circle meeting, I had another meditation at home, when I was told to look east towards the mountains. I saw my little cherub with a bow and arrow sitting on a cloud, and then I saw my Japanese spirit guide and the little boy, whom I had taken to be Chinese. My Japanese spirit guide told me that this was her son. She also told me that I would not be limited to automatic writing; that there would be many other spiritual areas that I would become involved with.

She also told me that it was not just coincidence that I had moved to this part of Spain, where I had made my home. I saw a vision of Sarah, a friend who was just getting over a stroke, surrounded with a purple, orange and yellow haze, and I was told that she was now recovering and that Jack was too. However, my friend, Emily, my guide said was not well. (Emily sadly died later that year). I was then told to play with the children.

I decided to attempt automatic writing once more when I was alone by myself. Again my hand flew across the page. The message I received was much more cohesive and spiritual than before and if it proved to be correct was quite mind-blowing. It read:

"Write upon elypally and go to hear and see and you will be in time. Messages yes. This is for Mike. He must be quiet and he must go to bed. He is getting old and his time will be soon. There is nothing to fear. Wait. There is a big balloon high in the sky waiting for him. What is there to fear, nothing. He will be happy. When you hear news you will know everything OK. Wait until you learn more. Keep listening. High in the mountains there is a goat with its head high listening. You will know when the time is right and then you must act. Lots of children around with lots of laughter and fun. They are happy. Good times. Grey lines around in the middle of the road. There is a circle to go round. No more messages. Elypally remains yours in time and year. Happy now."

CHAPTER 10

Helping Others through Healing

Our next Circle meeting marked another big turning point. First of all, Sarah, who had now significantly recovered from her stroke, joined us again and it was a very happy and emotional moment for us all welcoming her back. Secondly, this was the day that George was going to start explaining "healing" to us, and how we too could become spiritual healers.

George's credentials were quite impressive. He explained that he had himself started as a healer, then became a teacher, then set practitioner rules, and finally became an accreditation examiner. To be accredited, he explained, involved a very tough examination after two years of practice and this route was something that we could consider if we so desired.

George also explained the "code of conduct" governing all healers, in that everything a patient divulged should be kept strictly confidential, although with the passage of time we could obliquely refer to "successes" without naming the person concerned. He gave us many examples where he had treated patients with cancer and bone deformities who had stunned physicians afterwards, as their symptoms had completely disappeared. However, he stressed that after giving healing, we should always recommend that the patient see a "normal" doctor as well. Spiritual healing didn't always work, and he cautioned us not to become too involved, as we could take on the symptoms being treated.

We all watched as George gave a "hands-on" demonstration of healing for Sarah. At our next Circle meeting we would then learn to do this ourselves. Healing, he said, had nothing to do with clairvoyance. It was a means of spirits using our bodies to heal others.

We progressed on to giving each other clairvoyant messages.

Peter's message to me was that he saw me writing a book, something George had also seen a few weeks previously. George now felt certain that this message related to this book which I am writing at this moment, and of which they are both currently unaware.

After yet another enlightening evening, Mark asked me if I would try some healing on his knee. George was supportive of this request, but he cautioned me not to think of anything whilst I was doing the healing, so that I didn't inherit a bad knee as well!

Well, I tried the healing on Mark's knee and nothing worked!

CHAPTER 11

Elephally's Life in Libya

I continued to try my hand at automatic writing on two further occasions and received the following messages, the second of which is particularly interesting:

"Elephally in place for fund. Anything goes to what you get. Keep looking. Elephally will guide. There are stars in the sky and green fields. Messages yes. Tell you be careful you will be well. Healing helps everyone. Time and rest. Do not fret. Fine in time. Mark needs to go to hospital for cure. Everything OK. In past. There will be news of distant person. Wait until October. Broach, branch out and give help. Listen to the quietness and give peace. Do not struggle, hope to others. Line along river flowing fast. Speak to Gill she will have news for you. Go to heart for guidance. Keep looking after them. They are there in general but you will see. Listen to the silence when the time is right you will help others. I am going now. Elyphally."

"Hello I am elephally. I am pleased you are talking to me. I come from a far land by the sea. I come from Libya. Yes I had a large family. I had two daughters and one son. I was 78 when I died from old age and weary bones. I had a good life and I was very happy. I had two wives both lovely people. Keep trying you have much to learn and George will teach you. Listen. Keep writing.

When you hear you will write. Listen to me. Once you hear you will help others. You are starting to hear. Have patience. Mike October. Mark stays happy, tell him not to be afraid when he has his operation, everything will be all right. But he must go to be healed. Your brother is a strong man. He is going to travel and so will his family. He will live in a new country. His children will be happy. Keep in touch with him. When you elephally hear bells you will know. Time is important to everyone. Don't be sad you have much to do. Yes you will be given messages in time. Mother is smiling. Grandmother remembers in woods good friend your guide. Others want to speak. There are many voices around you. Your house is a happy house. It will help you with calmness and light. Elephally is going now."

I was particularly pleased with this last message as I had started talking to Elephally and asking him questions, a number of which he had now answered. The part about my grandmother was incredible, as I remember being lost in the woods with her and going behind a tree to ask my pretend friend for help in finding our way.

It was a number of weeks before I was able to attend another Circle meeting. That afternoon, before going to the meeting, I spoke to Elephally again and received the following extremely lucid and informative message:

"Hello I am here. I want to tell you about me. I was raised in the country on a small farm with ducks and other animals. We lived near water. The name of the village was Umidya in the south of Libya. We were a large family. No I did not continue to live on the farm. I went to Tripoli to find my fortune and became a tailor for many rich people. I was well respected and lived in a large house with my wife and children, their husbands and wives and grandchildren. I was very happy. No bad things happened to us, although others were not so fortunate. Some people disappeared never to be seen again. We were always looking out. There was much poverty and food was short. We used to eat a lot of fruits from the trees in our garden. My age was Mike, yes the same age. I am having difficulty with numbers. I was an old man. I used to wear

white tunics and a head band. I had an old car but the roads were not good and it broke down.

My house was behind a high wall and there was a fountain which the children played around. I used to sit and watch them as they made me happy. They used to get very dirty in the dust. I have been watching you carefully. I am glad we are making contact as there is much I want to share with you. I am with your family and friends and they are all happy for you.

Rona (my first husband's aunt) *wants to say hello, so does Hilda* (my maternal grandmother who I was in the woods with). *They are looking forward to having more contact with you. Keith* (my previous husband) *is also here. He is very happy for you and sends all his love. Cathy is here to.*

We all are very pleased to be able to talk to you and we are very excited. You will go to many places and see many people. Yes it will be to give messages. Yes I know you are having a hard time understanding this but you will learn and in time you will understand. What messages. Go to Elephally.

Look in the water for reflection. Elephally will show you. Look at the stars. There is a baby who will bring much happiness as she grows. Keep driving along the pathway even though it will be tough. The pathway to light. Green fields full of flowers. Happiness. Long walks good for you. Eat fruit from the land. Neighbours are there and will show you, like I did on my land. Peace is important. I am certain you will succeed. Keep trying. Go with caution, use the empathy you have to help others.

You must pass a message on. The message is for Mark from his son. He is waiting for him and Mark is very close to his heart. He has learnt much since passing. Keep close to other son, do not loose contact. Try harder and go to see him and tell him that you love him. This is very important. Do not drift, go soon. There is plenty to talk about and help him.

Message for Diane – well done. She will understand. Go tonight as there will be more discoveries for you. We are waiting. Tell George he is doing well for all of you and we will all be there to guide you along the pathway. Mark must be patient. In time he will hear and see his guides are there for him. He mustn't give up. It is written that Mark will follow, find his pathway. He will see the light. We are smiling with happiness for you all.

In the winter, in the snow, there will be a message for Jenny. She must wait for this. It will all be clear to her and she will be happy. I am getting tired now and need to rest for later.

Yours Elephally Umah"

When I arrived at the Circle meeting that evening, I showed George my latest messages and he was overwhelmed and urged me to continue a dialogue with Elephally. He said that he had been told that he would be receiving messages for us that evening, which indeed he did, as he went into a trance-like state.

He explained that like attracted like, and that no bad people would take us over when we became clairvoyant. There were "door keepers" protecting us. He asked Mark to envisage a blue light over him every other day, and to ask his spirit guides to come close to talk to him and to ask for healing. He said that Mark would soon have another spirit guide to help him. George asked me to imagine a green light over me when asking my guides to come forward. This was for calmness. He also said that I had two pathways to follow – automatic writing and mediumship – and that I should concentrate on both equally.

After George came out of his trance, he told Mark that there was a gentleman by him who had long off-white robes and a hood. He had grey hair and a beard and he would be there from now on to guide Mark. Mark accepted this and shortly thereafter said he had been told this was Ibrahim.

George then told us that we were going to try and use a pendulum to answer questions and find lost objects. He drew crosses on pieces of paper and gave us each one. He then swung his pendulum over the cross and asked his spirit guide to show him what indicated a "yes" and what meant a "no". Mark then tried to do the same using his wedding ring at the end of a piece of cotton. Slowly, the ring swung around signifying a yes, and in a straight line for no. I had absolutely no luck at all in getting my pendulum to move. Every time Mark asked his spirit a question the pendulum moved to answer yes or no correctly. This was a big encouragement to Mark, who had been feeling that he was not making any progress. It also showed that each of us had a different pathway to follow, and that Mark's was through the use of a pendulum.

CHAPTER 12

Previous Lives

I continued my dialogue with Elephally and received the following messages:

"When are you going to be in light? You must focus, you must see. I am going to find a way for you to see. Yes you did see me, but you will see more. You are in the countryside where it is very green. This is the right place for you. You will connect here.

Many moons ago you lived here. You were a young man working on the land but it was hard for you and you died young leaving a young family. You had four children and they too lived here for many moons. This is why you chose to settle here. You will stay here but not forever. You will move on to another place when the time is right. You will live for many moons it is your destiny to help others.

You will learn many things along your pathway. Look to the mountains and see the goats and the sun. Keep smiling. There are many things for you to see, we will show you. Yes there are many people here to talk to you but first you must go to the mountains. High in the mountains there is a small hut with views all around you. This is where you will find yourself.

Yes it is near to you. You will find it. You must talk more with us. We will guide you. It will be soon. Mark will be there too.

You have known him before in your past life. He will share you pathway with you. He will help you. You will find yourself. I am going now. Yours elephally umani."

This time Elephally has signed his surname slightly differently. I found his very old-fashioned way of using the English language and his spelling that was sometimes not quite right, very endearing!

This revelation however, that I had lived a previous life and that it had been close to where I lived now was astonishing. I was desperately keen to learn more.

My next attempt at communication with Elephally was even more interesting:

"Elephally will guide you. Elephally is here again with you. You are listening and you will see what you need to see. Look to the east to the sun you will see clearly over the water. There are many roads to be taken. Elephally is happy with you. You are calm and waiting for the sign. There is a message for your friend int you will out from under the tree she will go home. I am talking about your friend looking out towards the sea. She will travel a long way. There is a white hearth with a big fire welcoming her. This is warmth and hope for the future.

Mark will be here with you. You will learn together. He is a good man. He is the right one for you. You will be going on a journey and this will give you a new understanding. You will go to my country to the sun, white walls and covered ladies. You will be brave and ask many questions about me. I am there to guide you. Like the baby Jesus there will be a manger and a child who will talk to you. Look at his eyes.

You will look at a map and you will see where you must go. To the east. You will line elephally in eternal stone, you will line English, English person to this place in English house. You will be shown. You will be taken to this place for your learning. You will understand you must look at a map with your eyes they will see the place. It doesn't have trees it is in the dust but it will be home. Many moons will pass. Keep talking. You will discover many things.

Message for Chang watch your step. No more messages. The sun is coming out and there will be light for ever. You are safe and loved by your friends. Keep going to see George and listen to him."

And then another message:

"You are listening and you will find the shepherds hut. Yes it is in the mountains it is near you. You will know the way you have been there many times before. It is very quiet and peaceful. My house was very quiet, it was in the countryside, this is where I spent my childhood. Later I lived in the city. You should go to the city. You will find family called Umbuma. It is on the coast by the sea. It is a big house with a large tree outside the walls. You will see a picture of me.

But you must first find the hut in the hills and start your journey along many roads. You will receive messages from me to help you and others. The time will be soon you are getting there. But you must learn more. Do not hurry. There is plenty of time. You will see clearly what you have to do. Keep listening to the bells and see many moons in the sunlight. Rivers will flow past you and you will walk in the fields.

There are many happy faces around you on your journey. You will see more in time. I am showing you a coin it is shining in the sunlight it is pointing the way forward.

Look around you to the east and you will see old buildings. This is where you lived in your countryside. There is no-one living there now. It is in the mountains with the goats and the sheep and there is a river nearby flowing gently. Go soon and you will start to learn more.

I cannot tell you more now it is too early for you. Keep looking and listening. You are good. Going elephally."

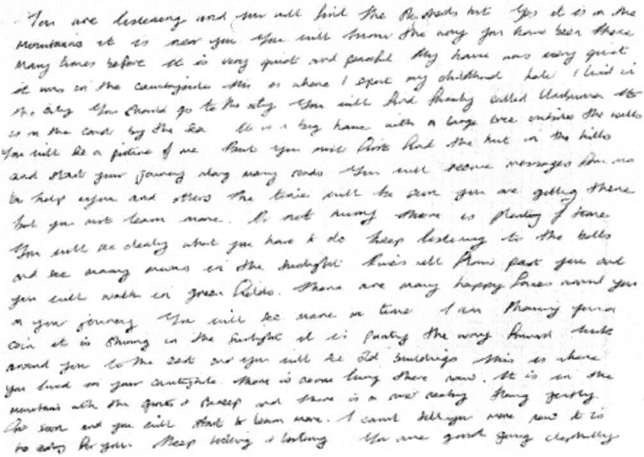

You are listening and you will find the [illegible] hut. Yes it is in the
mountains it is near you. You will know the way you have been there
many times before. It is very quiet and peaceful. My home was very quiet
it was in the countryside. This is where I spent my childhood. Later I lived in
the city. You should go to the city. You will find family called [illegible]
is on the coast by the sea. It is a big house with a large tree outside the walls.
You will see a picture of me. [illegible] you will [illegible] find the hut in the hills
and start your journey along many roads. You will receive messages from me
to help you and others. The [illegible] will be seen you are getting there
but you must learn more. Do not hurry there is plenty of time.
You will see clearly what you have to do. Keep listening to the hills
and see many [illegible] in the sunlight. Rivers will flow past you and
you will walk in green fields. There are many happy faces around you
on your journey. You will see more in time. I am [illegible]
[illegible] it is shining in the sunlight it is [illegible] the way [illegible]
around you to the east and you will see old buildings. This is where
you lived in your countryside. There is [illegible] living there now. It is in the
mountains with the goats & sheep and there is a river [illegible] flowing gently.
Go soon and you will start to learn more. I cannot tell you more [illegible] it is
[illegible] for you. Keep writing & looking. You are good going [illegible]

Each time I attempted automatic writing, the messages became clearer. The next one read:

"Hello, you are in the right mind and you will learn. You will find the hut. Yes you must go there. You will recognize it from your vision. It is important that you go there. You will start to see many things.

There is a ship in the bay, it is waiting for you. Listen to your heart. When you see the ship you will start your journey. When there are five in the clayside. Look at the stars. Alongside wisdom there is moderation. Wait for the sign. You will see in time golden apples in the harvest. There is a man who will ask you help. You must look at him and tell him to go home. There are people waiting for him. You are young and you need to grow more.

I see snow on the ground, all very white and there will be children singing for there is much to celebrate. All of you will see bright lights and find you can help others. When you go to George ask him as he will know. There is a big brown door to be opened with dogs waiting to go through.

Peter is finding his way and he knows of me. Ask him more about life in Libya (Peter, my fellow Circle member used to live in Libya as a child). *Look again at a map and find my village.*

The name is Mertaya Umbani in the countryside. Mantagne. It is in the south by water and desert. There are only rough roads and it is remote. Look to find my name, you need to know. You will find. I am happy. Elepally."

During one of my meditations I had clearly seen a ruin of an old hut/house in the mountains, so I now knew what to look for to start my journey.

I continued with my automatic writing and received this message. Elephally seemed to jump around in his reference to his house in Libya and my hut in the mountains, with a small boy:

"You must go to the house of mine. There will be many people there to speak to you. They are all waiting for the time is now right. You must tread carefully as there is much to tell others. In the valley there is a man waiting. He is alone in his thoughts. Just be there in time. Let him be.

Tell Jenny to listen to her thoughts. In time she must go to another place. It is right that she should do this. There is another world there for her with her family. They will look after her. She must not be afraid for she will be shown the way. Elephally wants you to help her. There will be another Circle for Jenny. You must stay in this "Circle" for George has much to show you.

Wait for the map and look in the south by water for my house. There were only a few houses here and it was very poor.

Look at the sky to the east past rivers and mountains. Look for the goats and a small boy with a big smile. Elephally sees all. There is a big wheel in the sky. Lady in house by river has much to see. Flowers are yellow in the fields. Big boots and many butterflies. Stony path with large rocks into the distance. Help is needed. Would find end of tunnel. This is difficult. Keep going and listening. Look for the chairs around a rug to welcome people.

You are happy. Elephally Umbani."

I scoured the internet to see if I could find Elephally's village but to no avail. I therefore decided to purchase a detailed map of Libya and keenly awaited its arrival so that I could do more research. The map duly arrived in the post and I decided to seek Elephally's help again through my automatic writing:

"Center by water. The place is Imbari and the village is Assuma, Awbari, Awbari. Yes that is it. This is the place where I lived. You must look further and find out more. I am very pleased. I said you must look at a map and that you would find the place. I am very excited.

Now you must find the hut in the mountains with the goats and the young boy. You have seen in your mind's eye a vision of the hut. It is high in the mountains. There is no one living there now. Take the path to the left and then to the right and carry on upwards to the sky. There is only a narrow pathway. When you get there you must pray for lives of your friends and yourself. This is your destiny and you are doing well. Keep looking and you will find.

There is a bridge over water and the sun is shining on the water. This is a good sign. There are many trees which are protecting you in your search. Tell Mark about the boat, that he will find his journey and to look at his fingers and his ring for they will tell a story to him. You are on your way. I am elephally umbani."

Looking at the map [6], I felt goose bumps on my skin as there is an area to the South of Libya called Idehan of Ubari where there is a village, Awbari (Obari). This was incredible and proof to me of Elephally's authenticity.

I also subsequently found photographs on the internet of the Ubari Lakes (Awbari) [7], exactly matching Elephally's description of where he lived.

CHAPTER 13

Lost Souls

Our Circle meetings seemed to be struggling, with all of us having difficulty in receiving clairvoyant messages. However, there had been a recent spate of tsunamis in the Pacific, where we reasoned the spirits would be spending much of their time helping those who had passed away during the storms.

At one of our meetings I had a strong feeling that I should mention those poor souls who were still trying to pass to the other side. George said that this was a subject that we would be tackling later. However, at this point Peter saw an American soldier called John Lawrence walking towards him, obviously trying to find his way. George immediately told Peter how to help this gentleman find "the light" and I was conscious of his passing to the other side.

Having now located Elephally's birth place in Libya, I decided the time was now right to try and find the shepherd's hut in the mountains. Early one Saturday morning Mark and I consulted a map of the area where I believed the hut would be found, and discovered an old cortijo, high up in the mountains. Cortijo in Spanish means "old farmhouse". We decided that we would try to find this place. Unfortunately, we never got as far as this cortijo. The pathway was incredible steep, stony and precipitous. We climbed for over an hour until we reached the skyline. I kept scanning the horizon to the east, looking for a hut, but the only evidence I could find that we might be on the right trail was lots of goat droppings on the path! I sat down on a rock to consult Elephally:

"You must continue along the path and keep looking out. Be careful as you go. You are home here. Look to the sky and go another way. You must keep looking along another pathway and you will eventually find the place. Go home and try again for you will find the hut in the mountains. Continue to look to the east."

Tired from our long walk, and disheartened that we had not found the shepherd's hut, we stopped off at a small bar at the base of the mountains, where we discovered plenty of photographs of the local area. Amongst the many photographs was a picture of a cortijo which looked vaguely similar to the one I was seeking, but which didn't quite match the vision I had seen.

However, there was a picture of another cortijo close by, which very much matched my vision – Cortijo El Paraiso.

On returning home I again referred to my map of the area and discovered that this cortijo was to the east, high in the mountains and close to a river. Might this be the place? I could see me getting very fit from many long walks before finding my hut.

Two days later and just before the Circle meeting I tried to contact Elephally again and received the following message:

"Keep looking. Yes I can help you. You must go the right and then to the left along the track to find the hut. You must find a new pathway. You will know the house when you see it. The name of the house is paraiso. It is by the river high in the sky. When you arrive there you will know that it is right. We are waiting for you and when you find it all will be clear to you. You will then start your own pathway and help others. You will write about it and others will believe you. Do not give up.

The others in the Circle will find their pathways which will be different to yours. Mark has a pendulum, Jenny a crystal ball, Peter his cards and Jessica can see into the future. Sarah will take time and will help others. You will be a teacher with many followers. You must keep seeking the truth.

Messages today in the Circle. Relax and listen to the silence. Many people in the sky helping this day including your dog. Look at the water and its journey to the sea. Let go and keep writing. I will tell you more later.

You must take bread and water to the fields when you look for the hut. It will be a long journey for you and you will need to rest. It is set on green pastures with space around it. Some of the roof has collapsed and in ruin. There is a young boy and a dog there waiting. They are playing outside the house. This is your guide. On the ground there are many rocks and flowers. It is very peaceful and this is where you lie. This was your life here and your soul will be awakened in the sun when you find your home. This is a journey that you must take for it will give you freedom. Do not be afraid.

You will help other souls find their way home when you find yourself. You will see a beach at night and will feel many people there. You must show them the light for their pathway. This will be how you will help others. You must learn to do this in time. The east is important. Look there. You will go there. Keep learning and looking. All will be clear to you.

Do not be disappointed today. The others will learn more and this is their pathway. You will see many people and help them along their pathway to the sun. This will be new to you but it is a skill that you already have and is the reason for you. I am an old man made happy and I have trust in you. Yours elephally unami."

Again, a slightly different spelling of Elephally's second name, but in essence the same. I was, however, incredibly excited when I saw the name "Paraiso" as it so closely matched the name Cortijo El Paraiso. I also reflected on the last Circle meeting when we had encountered a lost soul and helped him to find "the light" and to pass to the other side. Was Elephally's message telling me that this would be what I would be doing in the future?

At the Circle meeting that evening we had another two "guinea pigs"; two ladies unknown to us waiting for us to pass clairvoyant messages to them. George also gave me pen and paper and suggested that I also ask Elephally if he wanted to pass on any messages. As the others started to pass on messages, I felt my hand writing again with the following message for Lady Number 1:

"Little boxes, putting life into neat packages, sorting through things, throwing some things away, sifting as to what is important"

And for Lady Number 2, I wrote *"aero plane"* and *long journey.*

When it was my turn I passed on these two messages. Lady Number 1 apparently ran an auction house, for which the message was very apt, and Lady Number 2 had just undertaken a long plane journey.

For Lady Number 1, I also saw waterfalls with crystal clear water and birds in trees. I told her that she would be taking a new direction in her life and that this would give her new-found freedom; that she was being given red roses, indicating much love and support for her new life from a person on the other side and that this person greatly approved of what she was doing. As I was passing on the message I became very emotional, taking on the feelings of the person from the other side. This message was accepted by Lady Number 1.

All the others passed on incredible messages to the two ladies, of which about 95% were accepted.

A number of weeks passed before I was able to go to another Circle meeting, and the day before I decided to see if I could have a chat with Elephally. I received the following message:

"I go everywhere in the world and I see many things. You must let your mind travel to help others. There are many pictures to be seen and you will learn how to read these. Imagine a rock and see in it a house. Yes you can see it. There is a party with lots of people and a cloud comes over causing them to stop and look. What are they looking for? They are looking to see if they will have rain for their crops. They are happy and excited.

Life is very simple. Do not make it complicated. You can be happy with little, just enough food and your health.

You need to help people who are lost. You will hear them. Everyone needs to have faith and hope to have meaning in their lives and future lives. It will take time for you to find your house, but you are on your journey to understanding. Even Jesus had to learn how to help others.

In the morning you will go to George's and he will have messages for you. You still need to focus on the mountains and the hut high in the sky. There will be messages for others and they too seek to find their answers. Look, sit on the bench and you will be joined by an old man who will tell you of his childhood and how you can learn from this. I am an old man and I have seen many things that I will tell you about in time.

You must try again with the ball. You need to concentrate more and listen to the birds. In time all will make sense to you. You must keep learning and I will be there, as are your other friends. Go to see Lucy, she needs to talk to you.

You will discover more when you go to the East. There is a beach that is waiting for you. You will know when you have arrived. It will be at sunset and you will look out to sea and know that the time has come. You will see a young man running along the beach towards you with his arms flung wide. He will look like a monk with orange robes. Do not be afraid. I am tiring now and will talk you again soon. Elephally."

The next day I went to the Circle meeting which George started by saying that he had been receiving messages for all of us. He turned to me and told me that Elephally was a very important guide and that he was helping all of us in the Circle. Elephally had told him that I had been held back at the previous reading we had given to the two ladies, as the time was not yet right for me to develop my clairvoyance. Elephally wanted to lead me forward on another pathway first, concentrating on my writing, which he said would continue to provide great surprises, including the names of some famous people. In the future I would be able to develop my clairvoyance more and I would become a great medium.

We talked about the written message I had received the previous day, which George said had contained many symbols. House means "place of your heart". We also discussed the beach in the east and the monk running along the sands. I would be going to the East early the following year, to Thailand and Malaysia, and I strongly felt that my role in the future would be to guide lost souls to the other side. I asked George if he would be able to show me how to assist these lost souls find "the light" and their way to the other side.

Continuing with our meeting, George asked if we had any messages for the Circle. At this point I became very excited as I suddenly saw Elephally telling me that I too could pass on messages the same way as George. Elephally had long, grey shoulder-length hair and I suddenly realized that he was the guide I had seen previously, who was the spirits teacher (See Chapters 5 and 6). I stood up to tell everyone, and immediately burst into tears with emotion. I told everyone that Elephally was very pleased with all of us, as not only were we learning but we were also helping the spirits in the outer Circle around us to learn more about connecting with us. I said we should all be calm and that we would all receive increased wisdom, but most importantly that Elephally was delighted with us all.

George was thrilled with this message and particularly with the emotion that I had felt. He said that as I progressed I would find myself taking on the character of the person relaying the message. For example, if the spirit had a crooked arm, then my arm too would become crooked.

I felt as if I had turned yet another corner in my understanding of the spirit world.

CHAPTER 14

Finding my Previous Existence

The following day I visited Jenny, who lives in the national park, near where I believe the hut is that I am looking for. On the way we passed a track, which I felt I should take. Looking at a map, there appeared to be another track further into the national park which I could take, which would be a shorter route. Talking to Jenny, she confirmed that there was indeed such a track, and one that was drivable.

After leaving Jenny's house, I asked my husband if we could drive along the track to find the hut that Elephally had described. It was a very rough track leading high up into the mountains through pine woods. In the distance we could see an old house with part of the side without a roof. This was Cortijo El Paraiso (see Chapter 13) which Elephally had described. However, thinking back to my previous vision of what the hut should look like, this came close to my vision, except the ruined side without the roof should have been on the other side of the house.

We therefore continued along the track through the woods and shortly came across another old ruin, set high in the sky with a river running in the valley below. I felt instinctively that this was the place I was seeking, but asked Elephally for a sign. At this point I kept seeing Elephally in the sky around the building. I walked down to the river and looked back at the ruin, and it was outlined against the horizon, high in the sky as described by Elephally. This was Cortijo de Juan.

I felt very strange and decided to connect with Elephally through my automatic writing. This was what I wrote:

"Look down and you are here. This is where you lived your life. You had many sunsets here and were very happy. You lived off the land with your goats and chickens. Your children played here with their dogs. It was very quiet and very cold in winter. Look and you will see the trees. This will give you peace. You will now be able to continue on your journey of discovery.

As a young boy you used to walk many miles in the woods. The animals were your friends. There were many people who lived in your house, many generations. Your wife came from the other house and when you married she came to live with you in your house with your family where you had many children. Both families were very close. One day you had an accident and never returned home until now. You always wanted to be able to return.

Your wife lived to be an old woman and your children had many children. It was always a happy house with much love for everyone. You must now try to discover more yourself about this house and its people. You used to watch your wife washing clothes in the river and you never tired of looking up to the sky and watching the birds. It is good that you have returned. More will come to you as you think more about your journey. You have much to learn and this will be the start.

You lived there many moons ago when there were only donkeys to carry you along the pathway. Your wife's name was Maria and your name was Pedro Juan. You will have visions of your life if you concentrate. Look at the fireplace and see Maria with a baby in her arms and a shawl around her head. She had long dark hair which you loved to stroke. Your first born caused great happiness and celebration and you were very proud of yourself. You were only a young man yourself at seventeen years and your wife was fifteen.

You had four children who lived. Sadly three did not survive as it was a harsh and difficult place with no doctors around. Maria used herbs from the land to cure ailments. She had a very good knowledge beyond her years of the powers of herbs. She also had great insight into our world, the one beyond yours. Your children used to ride on a cart pulled by the donkeys – they could only just fit on it and used to wave to you. On big occasions you used to all visit the village for fiestas where you would dance and be merry. You can feel yourself standing on your land highlighted against the sky looking to the mountains, looking to the future, which is now. Think more and I will be with you guiding you along your pathway. I am yours elephally."

So this was Cortijo de Juan, where I had lived, not Cortijo El Paraiso. I suspected, however, that I had strong links with Cortijo El Paraiso as well.

This was also the second time that Elephally had referred to my having had four children and to my having had an accident.

CHAPTER 15

My Long-Lost Family

I spent ages looking on the internet to see if I could find any further information. The only thing I could find was that the names Pedro Juan and Maria are common to the area.

The following day I telephoned Jenny to tell her about my discovery and to ask if she could speak with some of her neighbours in the National Park to verify all that I had been told by Elephally and to find out how long ago people had lived in this house. Jenny was as excited as myself and said she would immediately go out to talk to her neighbours.

At the same time I also telephoned George, who asked if I had gone inside the ruin. This was important, he said, as it would have completed my task of finding the hut and that I would now move on along my pathway of clairvoyance; that things would start moving a lot faster for me now.

Two things then happened. First of all, Jenny called me to say that the person who owned the house near Elephally's (where my wife in my previous life had originated) was called Maria (the same as my wife's).

In Spain, it is very common for the daughters to take the name of their mothers.

Staggeringly, she also told me that the person who owned the ruin that I had found was in fact my neighbour. This sent shivers down my spine, as the implication was that this neighbour could be my son, grandson or great-grandson! And what a coincidence that I should now have him as my closest neighbour.

Secondly, I showed George a photograph of Cortijo de Juan, which he felt a strong connection to. He said that many people had lived in this house at the same time, and for many, many years: probably for at least the last couple of centuries. Also, the original house had been extended. We agreed that all the Circle members should visit this Cortijo to see how this could help them along their pathway, particularly as it is probably no coincidence that we are all part of the same Circle.

Remembering the part of my message from Elephally about sitting on a bench and listening to an old man, I tried to meditate focusing on a bench. I immediately found myself sitting on a bench by a table covered with a red and white check table cloth. There was an old man there offering me bread and red wine. When I related this to George, he told me that this signified that the old man was offering me his hand of friendship.

Sunday morning dawned bright and clear, as I prepared myself to visit our neighbours to ask about the ruin I had visited. I was feeling particularly nervous in my pursuit of the truth. If they could tell me nothing then I would feel disappointed and if they could verify any of the information Elephally had given me, then I would be blown away.

I received the normal warm effusive greeting from my neighbour's wife and her brother and sister, who were now in their late 80's. After chatting for a while, I decided to broach the subject of Cortijo de Juan, and to my surprise found that it had belonged to my neighbour's wife's grandfather and his wife (Antonio and Carmen) who had last lived there some seventy to eighty years ago. Her father was Benito, and her brother and sister, who were sitting in front of me, were two of

Benito's seven children; the others were called Miguel, Alfonso, Pedro, and Arturo. My neighbour's wife had moved into the house next to ours when she married her husband. She and her brother and sister all had fond memories of Cortijo de Juan. It was apparently over two hundred years old.

My neighbour confirmed that her grandfather would have lived off the land from his chicken, goats, crops such as peppers, potatoes and tomatoes, and fruit from the trees. There was also an abundance of herbs, which they would have used for medicinal purposes as well as for cooking. There were no fish in the river but it was used for washing, albeit it was extremely cold in the winter.

The track to the nearest village was also very dangerous in parts and donkeys were used wherever possible as it was a long walk. Seventy to eighty years ago, however, there were many people living close by. My neighbour kept referring to Cortijo Castaño, which she felt was also called Cortijo El Paraiso. Maybe she was indicating some sort of connection between the two Cortijos.

So the burning question was, is my neighbour's grandfather, Antonio, my son? Something had happened to Antonio's father that they could either not remember or were unwilling to discuss – that father might have been me! The names Pedro Juan and Maria sadly meant nothing to my neighbour, her brother or her sister.

The next Circle meeting proved to be another turning point for us all. George opened by saying that as Elephally had already raised the subject he would like to talk about reincarnation. He said that a spirit had the choice as to whether they wanted to return, but normally this would not be until they had passed over for more than fifty years. He said that he did not agree with hypnosis to explore past lives as this interfered with the information being passed to us by our spirit guides. However, he did agree with regression if this was done carefully.

Unfortunately, not all the Circle members were present at this particular meeting, which meant that our spirit guides were holding back on our next stage of development until we were all present. To prepare for this, George wanted to assess at what stage we all were on our spiritual path, and asked us to all focus on a flower.

When relating his meditation, which had centred on a sunflower, my husband Mark burst into tears, as his meditation had led him into a room with all his relatives, and he had talked to each one. He was very overcome by emotion from the contact he had been given.

Throughout the Circle meeting I had been looking at George's crystal ball, which had been placed on his sideboard. I saw a young baby trying to walk with an outstretched hand behind it. I stood up and said that we were all this child. We had all been struggling to find our feet, but had now found them and were progressing into another stage of our development. I felt that we should all visit the Cortijo that I had found the previous week, as I felt this was a discovery for all of us from which we had much to learn; that there was something at this site for all of us.

Mark's message to the Circle was incredible. He stood up and just talked, with words flowing from him. He felt that normally he would never have been able to be so fluent and coherent and felt that someone else was speaking through him. It was all about us trying and taking a step at a time.

CHAPTER 16

More about my Previous Life

A couple of days after the Circle meeting, I felt the need to communicate with Elephally again so that I could ask him about my children and any connection with my neighbour. I had remembered that back in July (see Chapter 9) Elephally had told me that my neighbours would help. He had also made reference to looking towards the horizon and seeing the light and that I should keep looking towards the mountains as this would be where I would find what I was looking for. But I am getting ahead of myself now.

I then wrote the following:

"You are doing well. The time is now right and there is much for you to learn. It is a good idea to check records of who lived in your house so that you can learn about your family. The names of your children were Rosa, Louisa, Antonio, Pedro, Pepe, Juan and Maria. The names of your children who died were Pepe, Juan and Louisa.

Antonio and Pedro continued to live in the house but your two daughters married and went to live with their husbands. Antonio and Pedro had children and their children had children as well, they are the ones that are still living. Yes Antonio is your son and your neighbour is your family.

Yes go back to the hut with your friends as they too have much to learn. You should all listen to the quietness and find your own pathways. I will be their guide and help them too. They have nothing to fear.

You must look at the sky and the birds and remember. You will now find new things. Look for a stile, like a bench across the river. You are pleased to have returned home. Go inside again and feel my presence. Take George with you as he too will feel many things. Jenny is on her own journey. She too came from nearby. There is a dog waiting for you, he has been waiting for your return and has missed you.

Think more about your life, both now and in the past. It will help you to help others discover more about themselves. In time you will discover many things. Keep looking for signs like the apples you used to enjoy. Look at the river and the water, see in it a reflection. Yes, church but do not be disappointed, there is little to find. Look along other pathways as you will now pass on to another journey of understanding. I am proud. Elephally."

I was a little sceptical about this message and wondered whether my own knowledge had influenced what I had written, particularly the reference to Antonio, as this was the name my neighbour had given me as the last person to live in the Cortijo (her grandfather and my son?).

I had arranged for all of us in the Circle to visit the Cortijo high in the sky, but unfortunately three of the Circle dropped out for various reasons. This left just Jenny, Mark and me. Before leaving that morning I again had a message from Elephally:

"It is good that you will be returning. I will be there waiting for you. You must look around you for all that I have told you, particularly look for your dog. Wander into the house so that you can feel the presence of those who lived there. Many people lived there after you. You will make new discoveries. Keep looking and listening to the birds.

Yes you had 7 children. Yes you had a son called Antonio, who lived to a great age with his wife and family. The names of Antonio's children were (Indecipherable) and Pepito. Ask Jenny for more names. Go now and see the hut and the river. Try to see if you can find your memories. Talk to yourself and stand on the hill listening to the birds. Try to focus and listen to what you hear. Use the strength of your friends so that they too will find guidance along their pathways. Remember that your pathway will not be easy, you need to take your time and listen to what I have to say. All will become clearer to you. Yours elephally."

It was a lovely, crisp, autumnal day as the three of us drove into the mountains. I decided not to tell Jenny of the last two messages, and instead asked her to let me know if any names came to her whilst we were visiting the Cortijo. On our arrival the three of us all walked in different directions.

I decided to go back inside the Cortijo, and as directed by Elephally prayed for my friends and for myself. I then closed my eyes and saw a dog with long floppy brown and off-white coloured ears bounding towards me in happiness, closely followed by a young boy with black hair. The three of us clung together and walked towards the sun, a vast bright light which we disappeared into.

I continued looking around the inside of the house, and on seeing Jenny sitting quietly in one of the rooms, I decided to walk out to the land around the house and sat down, amongst the herbs, listening to the birds and the gurgling of the river, to see if Elephally would write any more to me:

"Yes you are looking and you are seeing. Your dog is very happy now that he has gone to the sun with you and your son. They have waited a long time for your return. Imagine what it was like when you lived here. There were many fruits to eat from the land and you had many animals which you used to walk with. Sometimes with your son Antonio. You were very happy together. This was your favourite child as he was your first born. Look to the right and see into the distance, this was the way you used to walk to your friends. There is so much peace for you here. Listen to the birds and their song. You can feel children around you and your father, who was getting very old. Feel the wind around your face in the sun and know that you have peace and happiness.

In the summer you would eat here with your children and watch them running around playing games. Your girls had long dresses and your boys little waistcoats and knee length trousers and little caps, like a tea cozy. Look for a bread oven where you wife used to make bread for you. Listen to the water from the river and go to see it."

I then paused and looked towards a pile of stones, which I felt was my grave. I walked over to this part of the land, which looked out over the river and to the mountains beyond, which was towards the east. I felt great emotion and wanted to cry. So I consulted Elephally again:

"Yes, this is where you are buried and it is only you are now feeling great sadness as you look out across your favourite view. You used to sit here for many hours just looking and listening to the birds and the water. Know that you have now found yourself and can be released to carry on. You can see the river from here and hear it. Seeing the dam emerge as a powerful light in the sky."

At this point I asked both Mark and Jenny to stand where I felt I was buried to see if they received any feelings. I didn't at this point tell them why.

Mark said he had a feeling of heaviness and saw people and animals running around.

Jenny then told me what she had seen whilst sitting in the cottage (as she called it). She saw a young woman. Her hair was parted in the middle and it was tied back and long. She saw a slight young man and questioned why she should be able to see this young man, and she got the feeling that this was possible as she was seeing another spirit. The young man had a pudding basin haircut. It was October and time for the harvesting of the grapes (which were purple, not green). He was sporting (although it was not cold but to please Maria), a leather hat which she had made him from sheepskin. It was a simple hat turned back at the brim, similar to the waistcoat that the man was wearing.

The young man then left to hunt rabbit. He walked down to the river, crossed to where the river used to flow to the right and followed the path of the water to set snares. He walked up high into the inlet and was startled by something (maybe a wild pig) and slipped into a cavern and was not able to get out.

Maria knew the direction in which he had walked and spent days looking for him but he never returned.

Jenny then said she saw Maria and the children at what would have been Christmas time, all looking very sad and acting out a play, with the young man in spirit watching them.

I then told Jenny that I felt as if I was standing on my grave and I was conscious that I was looking towards the ravine that Jenny had described. I read out to her the message I had received from Elephally and when I mentioned the name "Antonio", there was a short intake of breath from Jenny. She said that only one name had come to her whilst meditating and that was Antonio!

I now knew how I had died and it was incredibly emotional. I also knew that I had just returned to the light with my son and dog and that that chapter in my previous life had now been closed.

The three of us left the Cortijo and stopped off on the way home at the bar in the national park for a late lunch. I looked again at the photographs in the bar and saw one of my Cortijo, Cortijo de Juan. There was another photo of a different Cortijo, and below that a photo of Cortijo El Paraiso, except that the caption was for Cortijo Castaño (the name of the Cortijo that my neighbour had been referring to).

Jenny and I asked the barman where Cortijo Castaño was situated, and found that it was located close to Cortijo de Juan, so this would have been the nearest Cortijo to me. Jenny said that she had tried to find Cortijo Castaño previously, but because she was with other people had turned back on their walk before they reached it. She had felt quite dejected at the time and was keen to have another attempt at finding it. We agreed that we would try again a couple of days later. Maybe this was where Jenny had lived in her previous life?

At the next Circle meeting we all related our experiences at Cortijo de Juan and showed the other Circle members photographs. George, when he looked at the photographs, told me that the date of 1820 would be significant. On checking the internet I discovered that the Spanish Civil War raged between 1820 and 1823. So George's date of 1820 did have significance.

George also told me that my automatic writing would continue and that many famous people would be writing to me through Elephally. So there was still more to come?

A few days later, Jenny, Mark and I set off again to find Cortijo Castaño. The first track we tried came to an abrupt end, and just as we were about to turn back, Mark spotted another ruined Cortijo nestled in the mountains to our right. We trudged back to the main track, got in the car and drove back along the track looking for another track, which sure enough we found. The track led us through some beautiful forested scenery across a small dry river bed. Finally, rounding a corner, we came across yet another ruined Cortijo. The setting of this Cortijo was truly magnificent, with stunning views looking down across the river valley, but it was obviously not the one we were looking for. Looking to our left, we could see the other Cortijo we had seen from the previous track. This Cortijo, which was obviously Cortijo Castaño, looked down on the same river bed as the Cortijo I had lived in, in my previous life. My Cortijo was also visible in the distance.

All three of us tried to meditate to see if we received any messages, but disappointingly none of us did. I just had the distinct impression that this was where Maria had lived as a child.

I returned home and felt the need to communicate with Elephally again. I wrote the following:

"You have found your pathway. You went along it yesterday high into the mountains. The other two houses belonged to the family of Maria, where her parents lived. Your wedding was in the Spring when the first flowers were bursting into bloom and Maria had flowers in her hair. It was a big celebration bringing together two families, who had suffered many losses during the war. Your houses were built high in the sky to afford sanctuary and security and for you to be able to see troops approaching so that you could hide in the hills. Your fathers were very loyal men but they only had very basic arms to fight with and they were both killed. It was a very sad time and your wedding signified a new life starting again.

It was in 1820 that your father went to fight but it was not until much later that he was killed. He held you in his arms before he left. It was a very hard life and his brothers helped to raise you. You never stopped looking at the ravine and the water bed below to ensure no one threatened your family again. You all felt very secure living high in the mountains and there was always enough food for you all.

You will always feel at home here as you have found your roots with the past. Now you must carry on forward and discover your new pathway and journey which will take you to different lands and different people. You have come back to help them. You already know where you must go. It is no coincidence that you have choice places for celebrations. Think of the East and return. More is waiting for you to discover. Do not struggle. Wait for the sunset and the beach and you will know what to do. Think about your doorway and the gardens beyond going into the sunlight. Do not be afraid. I am with you. Do not struggle to understand as I will explain when the time comes. Go in peace. Elephally."

There it was – the date of 1820 – was this coincidental, or had I been conscious of that date and had it affected my writing?

Elephally had successfully guided me along my pathway to discovering my roots and my previous life in the mountains of Spain. George had proved to be a wonderful teacher and guide in helping me discover my abilities as a medium and clairvoyant and in helping to guide others to finding the light.

Yet Elephally was promising still more for me to discover. I had learned a good deal about my spirit guide, Elephally, and I had established a genuine rapport with him. I was therefore keenly looking forward to continuing my journey and finding yet more new pathways and discoveries with Elephally's help, albeit it with some trepidation.

What did my future have in store for me, and would I be able to help others find the light? Time alone and Elephally will tell.

CHAPTER 17

Guiding Lost Souls to the Light

It was some time before I went to another Circle meeting, which marked yet another turning point. During our meditation, we were asked to focus on a book, to open it and to read the words in the book. This was to be a focal point for many Circle meetings to come. We all saw the writing in the book, and we were all able to read parts of the text. We all also found that we were able to go into trance-like states and to pass on messages from the spirit world.

I knew that my next challenge would be to focus more on developing my clairvoyance. I felt that there were many challenges ahead for me and that my forthcoming holiday to the Far East would feature prominently.

However, it was still a few months before that holiday, with Christmas approaching rapidly. Because of Christmas we had a long gap between our Circle meetings. Just before the next Circle meeting I had a vision of a white camel, with a nomad sitting on it with a wrap around his face, so that I could only see his eyes. I concentrated and was given the name Sayeed. He told me that he would look after me in his country.

A few days later I decided to try to meditate and chose to knock on the door of a cottage. The door was opened by the same rotund lady with the frilly white hat and apron that I had seen before. She took me into the kitchen where, sitting around the table, were all my guides – Elephally, Nero (my Roman soldier), my Japanese lady and her son, Ben the monk and my new guide Sayeed. They told me that I had much work to do in the East and when I asked if I had further work to do in the mountains close to me, I was told no. I had shown my son in my previous life and my dog the way to the light, and this had been my lesson so that I could help many other lost souls in the East. I asked if Sayeed had appeared for a purpose and was told that he would be my guide to find Elephally´s house in Libya. Sayeed also gave me a very pale pink rose – the symbol of spiritual love.

Our next Circle meeting was held at my house, which is an old Cortijo (farmhouse), buried in the countryside. George and Anne were late arriving, but as Mark, Jenny, Sarah and I waited, we were all conscious of many spirits present in the room. I felt as if they were all crowding in and waiting for us to start. I saw Sayeed on his camel with first my monk holding the reins and then Elephally, with one hand holding the reins and the other leaning on a walking stick. I particularly felt that someone was sitting on the arm of my chair, with an arm around me, and Jenny told me there was an Indian lady there, who followed me when I went out of the room to let George and Anne in and returned back to the room with me.

Our Circle meeting was very relaxing. George said that we all had much to learn this year and asked us all to use our clairvoyant powers and give the Circle a message. He said it was very important not to think about the message before we stood up, but just to start speaking so that words would flow. When it was my turn I stood up with a completely free mind. I started by saying that I had seen all the spirits crowding around and I then found that I just kept talking, mainly about how we had to listen intently to what was being said because we would have to interpret what the spirit´s messages were, and that we should also look and see more clearly. I also found that I was able to pass on messages to my fellow Circle members.

After the meeting I told George about my meditation when all my guides had told me that I had work to do in the East. He told me that I must not be afraid (which strangely enough I was not) and that I was more powerful than my guides and that they were all gathering to help me along my path. He told me how to guide lost souls to the light and to the next world, but also told me not to expect too much. However, I was becoming quite excited and ready for my next challenge.

I set off for my holiday in the Far East with a feeling of anticipation and excitement. Would anything happen? Would I have any spiritual encounters?

On arriving on the island of Koh Lanta, Mark and I got up early every morning for a walk along the beach. One Monday morning we chose a different path, way off the normal tourist route, which took us through scrub land close to the sea. It was very peaceful and all we could hear were the birds and the ocean. Then suddenly we came across a graveyard with wooden pegs sticking up from the ground. I knew instantly that this was an area that had been affected by the tsunami disaster of 2004. The ground was scattered with tree stumps, the trunks of the trees had been torn away by waves and in amongst all this were parts of boats. It was an eerie feeling.

I immediately closed my eyes and felt an incredible presence around me. I saw a young woman coming towards me wearing a long sarong skirt and holding a small child in her arms, balanced on her hip. I felt instinctively that she was a lost soul and had been killed during the tsunami. I told her to look towards the light and watched her and her son float towards it, to join their loved ones on the other side. I also prayed for other lost souls who had also lost their human lives and felt a great rush sweeping past me, as these souls too headed for the light. It was an amazing feeling.

I went back to our hotel and asked Elephally if he would make contact with me. I received the following words:

"And you will see through the mist of time many things. You will be guided to the place of the sun and you will be given directions

along the way. The time is now right for you to see many more things. You must walk along the sands at sunset and look towards the sun and see the birds and the boats and the people waiting for you. Look at yourself and you will see another person. Look at the water and the reflections of life. Walk along the sand and do not be afraid. We are with you, we are your guides. Keep looking and you will see us. Be happy that you have been given this chance. Do no look back keep, going along the path, look for the keys. Go soon at sunset. You will find a young boy who will hold your hand and smile. Look at the children. Go with your heart for you will learn and see much in this country in the East. Wait and listen, close your eyes and you will hear. Go now."

Nothing else happened until quite a few weeks later when we were on the island of Koh Lipe. At sunrise we were walking along the beach, when three Buddhist monks, clad in orange robes, walked towards and past us. I was immediately reminded of my vision that I would see a monk in an orange robe walking towards me on the beach. I again closed my eyes and prayed for any lost souls, telling them how to find the light, but this time I didn´t feel anything.

Was I being too sceptical or trying too hard? Were there just too many coincidences for comfort?

CHAPTER 18

Moving past Senior School into College

And so it was a month later, before going to my next Circle meeting, that I again communicated with Elephally, telling him that I would be at the meeting that afternoon. Again he guided my hand over a piece of paper with the following:

"When you are looking you will see. We are with you. There is an envelope with information in it for you. This will be important. Do not dismiss it. Let yourself feel the vibrations. You will find your way to more information. Go to the Centre, keep looking.

Think positively. You will go slowly along your pathway. Now is the time to reflect on what you have seen and done. When you have learnt your lessons you will carry on forward. Think about what you saw and felt. Don´t forget the boat between the cliffs on the lake. Think about the monks and what they mean. You felt the silence and the solitude. Remember these feelings and use them in the future. There is much kindness to be seen. Think about the bright flames in the sky floating upwards. Never ignore what you see. We are here to show you the way. Reflect and be happy where you are. Elephally".

Elephally's messages were certainly becoming more spiritual and profound.

George started the Circle meeting this time by saying that this year we had all entered a different phase of our understanding. We had moved up past senior school into college, and this was our year. The major difference was that we would no longer need to do meditations; now we would be using clairvoyance by clearing our minds and opening a channel for the spirits to communicate with us and, through mutual trust, we would receive their messages. He said that the point of meditating previously was to ensure that our vibrations were on an even keel, so that the spirits could communicate with us. It was important therefore to relax and ensure that our vibrations continued to be on a calm level, so that our guides could speak to us. Symbols, he said, would play an even bigger part in communication from now on.

He told me that Elephally had been communicating with him all morning and that we would be learning something new that afternoon. When I told him that I had also been speaking to Elephally that morning, he said that Elephally had been speaking to us both at the same time. I told George about the automatic writing message that I had received that morning and the words "we are all with you", were ones that had been given to George too. And I had been told to "feel the vibrations", which George had just gone to such lengths to talk to us about.

George went on to say that "trust" had now been established between Elephally and myself. He had told me a little about himself and his life in Libya, which I had been able to verify, and also he had told me about my previous life, which I had also been able to verify. From now on, Elephally had told George, my automatic writing would progress, and during the course of the next year other spirits would make contact and I would be amazed at the messages coming through. I might even use these "writings" to write a book to inspire and help others!

Slowly, the meaning of my last two writings began to mean more. I interpreted this as follows:

Interpretation

And on your journey you will see many things. You will be guided to the golden light and you will be given directions along the way. The time is now right for you to see many more things. You must walk along the sands at sunset and look towards the golden light so that the people who are waiting for you will have freedom – their boats will be coming home and something nice will happen to them – they will be helped towards the golden light. Look at yourself and you will see another person. Look at the healing and the reflections of life. Walk along the sand and do not be afraid. We are with you, we are your guides. Keep looking and you will see us. Be happy that you have been given this chance. Do not look back, keep going along the path, look for the keys to solve your problems – you will open a door to opportunity, to new things and there will be success in what is undertaken. Go soon at sunset. You will find a young boy who will hold your hand and smile. Look at the children. Go with your heart for you will learn and see much in this country in the East. Wait and listen, close your eyes and you will hear. Go now.

When I closed my eyes and listened, I heard the whoosh of souls rushing to the golden light.

It was, however, the second piece of automatic writing that I found more profound. The reassurance was there that my guides were with me, helping me along my pathway. Would the envelope, which signifies big things, or an official paper, have information for me from the physical world, or information from them? They had told me to feel the vibrations, so that I could receive their messages ("you will find your way to more information"). "Go to the Centre, keep looking." Did this mean go to my inner core? And yes, now is the time for me to reflect as I find myself now doing this. Don´t forget the boat (boat coming home, something nice) between the cliffs on the lake (healing). The flames in the sky I am sure referred to lanterns that had been lit on beaches in Thailand which floated up into the sky – again, was this helping lost souls? I remember well my feelings of peacefulness and hearing the complete silence around me. Have I now learned my lessons so that I can carry on forward?

What I don't know is the significance of the three Buddhist monks, clad in orange robes, walking towards and past us on the beach, a vision of which I had previously seen.

Our next Circle meeting took a different turn. As George said, we had moved past meditations. He explained that at the previous week's meeting Jenny and Jessica had both gone into trances and had been able to pass on messages. Today, he again asked us all, in turn, to stand up and just talk; not to think about what we were going to say but to wait for words to be given to us.

Mark was the first to stand and he reminded us all of the need to relax so that the spirits could tune into our vibrations – something George had forgotten to say to us. The others all passed on messages and then it was my turn. I stood up and found myself saying that Elephally wanted to reiterate what he had told me that morning; that we should reflect on what we had learned so far, so that we could now progress and find our pathways, which we still had to determine.

George then asked us all to take it in turn to stand up and pass on a message to one of the Circle. Peter told me that I was tired, that I was thinking too much and that I should take time to walk in the fresh air and relax. Mark was again very impressive with the message he gave Jessica, all of which meant something to her. When it was my turn I felt I had a message for Peter. I saw a stone wall, then a well with a water bucket and then a dog beside the well. I asked Peter if this meant anything to him, as I felt that these were symbols, which should be interpreted. George helped me out by explaining that the wall signified the block of understanding that Peter had found himself against, the well signified healing and a new beginning, and the dog signified his faithful spirit friend helping him along the way. Peter saw a large diamond for me. Again, George interpreted this as being "multifaceted". He said that this would apply to my automatic writing, where I would expand into different areas – this he said was the message from Elephally to me.

CHAPTER 19

Proof and Prophecies from Elephally

A number of Circle meetings followed where I felt that I wasn't really progressing, although George kept reassuring me that I was becoming more clairvoyant. If I were truthful, the Circle meetings were beginning to bore me and on a couple of occasions when George was talking, I fell asleep on the sofa! At one meeting George told me that Elephally was missing contact with me and that I should start my automatic writing again. He said I would be extremely surprised by some very famous people getting in contact with me.

So the following day I sat down quietly in my lounge with pen poised, and made contact with Elephally. This is the message I received:

"Hello again. It has been a long time since we last talked and a lot has happened around the world. You have been listening and taking your time, which is good. Now it is time to start again with your writing. Imagine a small boy sitting beside a tree in the fields. There is nothing around him, only silence and he is waiting. What for? He is waiting for a second coming. He is preparing himself

for the light, as you must do as well. You will see warriors coming towards you. They have painted faces, grass skirts and wooden spears. This is the advance. They are coming to protect you and guide you. Masai warriors, you will hear. They are strong, peaceful and happy. Do not be afraid for they will help you and prepare you for what will follow. There will be a huge gust of wind as you feel the new presence. You will feel uplifted and gain a new knowledge. You will be ready. Look at the book of life and be ready to spread the message. There will be alarm but you will calm this. Cross the river, keep the sun on your face. Light candles.

Go to the West and seek out an old man, who will be your guide. You will recognise him when you see him. There will be footprints to follow. There will be danger but you will overcome this and continue. Do not listen to those who do not understand. You will be guided and you will know what to do. Go in peace and feel happy for you have much to learn and experience. You are only a child. Look into space, at the larger prospective and the night sky. Imagine yourself up there looking down at the beautiful things around. Man has lost the ability to appreciate what he has been given. He needs to learn to love his life, as it is very precious. He needs to change his perspective and to love others around him. Man is creating too many bad things in your world and this has to be stopped. It will be stopped for man's survival.

You will start to help to make a difference. Keep in touch and keep looking with your eyes open as you will see the signs and the old man who is patiently waiting for you. Do not think this is crazy. It is your destiny. It will happen. Do not be surprised when changes occur. They are written; they were written many moons ago. Feel peaceful and listen to the birds. Give yourself time, relax and look outwards. Have empathy and kindness for simple things. Make a difference. Go with God. Elephally".

Well, this was certainly more profound than any previous writings of mine. A few weeks' later, shortly after the 2010 UK General Election, when there was a hung parliament and I was still waiting to hear who would be the next Prime Minister, I decided to try my writing again. The Election results in the UK were furthest from my thoughts, so the words that now follow were incredible:

"Listen to what you hear. Listen to the breeze as there are many voices to be heard. Listen and feel. See the dark rider on his horse galloping towards you from the distance. He is bringing news with him to help you and others. He has journeyed far and he is getting weak but he is determined that you should hear what he has to say. Look and you will see that he has arrived and is walking towards you with his arms and hands outstretched. This is his greeting to show he comes with peace. You can now see the smile on his face and he is sitting close to you. Take your time.

I have come a long way to be here today. This is the right time for you to hear me. There are many of your followers and friends who want to talk to you as they are all concerned about what is about to happen and to help you on your pathway to helping others. The world is following a pathway, that they do not understand. They do not feel it is the correct way and there will be much distress before changes can be made. You must be strong and stay here as you will be shown the way to help. There is much unrest in the world and your people need to understand that they cannot have everything. They must work for their rewards. Mankind has been given life and they should treasure this and not take it for granted. They have lost sight of the simple things that make happiness. They have become too greedy in their expectations.

You will see that soon there will be people wishing to change things, to help the world become a better and safer place. You do not understand at the moment how you can help, but you will. Now my journey has been worthwhile. My name is Ethred. I must go now and return to my home, for I have been away a long time waiting for this moment. I would like to thank you and wish you well for your future tasks.

The lady is here with her baby (the one I saw in Thailand and guided towards the light). *She is very happy. She will be there to help you. Tennyson is also close and so is Gladstone. Do not be afraid. Gladstone is very amused by what is happening in your country. He says not all is decided yet and you will see many silly people trying to better themselves first before the good of your country. These people will not last because this is the greed that I have mentioned. There is one good man who will take control and lead the way out of your country's problems. He has yet to become known but he is there in the background slowly helping to ensure the right direction is taken. He is a man from the north of your country and he is wise beyond his years. We have chosen him to come forward to right the wrongs.*

Tennyson is my right arm. He has wit and intelligence and will talk you later. When you look you will see many people coming towards you. They are the poor and crippled. They are also holding out their hands and walking towards you as quickly as they can. They will be guarding you. Feel the peacefulness now as times are changing. Do not be unhappy for there is much brightness ahead for you as you take your new journey. Think about who you are meeting and learn quickly from them. You need to smile more and be happy. This is your destiny. We will talk again soon. Elephally."

After receiving these messages I decided to look on the internet to see if there was any connection between Tennyson and Gladstone, and what I discovered was quite incredible. Gladstone and Tennyson were both born in the same year (1809) and died within six years of each other. Tennyson went to Cambridge a few months before Gladstone went to Oxford. Tennyson accepted "a peerage in 1883 at Gladstone's earnest solicitation." "He took his seat in the House of Lords on 11 March 1884."[8] There was the undeniable link between the two.

Well, no party won the General Election outright. Instead, a coalition government was formed between David Cameron of the Conservatives and Nick Clegg from the Liberal Democrats, neither of whom came from the North. So who is the man from the north, wise beyond his years?

Not long after, I again found the urge to try my automatic writing. George, being an accredited Spiritualist Minister, had called me the previous evening to ask me if I would ask Elephally to help him officiate at a wedding the following day. George was nervous in case he couldn't find the correct words to use. The following day I put pen to paper:

"Let us take a look at what you are seeing. You are starting to see more clearly and to understand what you see. Let us take an example. You are driving along in your car and you see an ox and an old man walking slowly along the road. This is no ordinary old man. He is wizened from the elements and yet he enjoys his walk with his ox. The ox is his friend and they communicate with each other. They watch what passes them by and know that life may be much faster now but it has not changed. You are still the same people but you need to be more content and more aware of the damage you are causing by your greed. Life should be simple. Take the old man and the ox as your guide.

George will have enjoyed his wedding. He will have found the right words to say as we have been close and helping him. Thomas is very happy. Tell him.

You are very happy. I am pleased to see you so. You have much to be happy about. Feel the happiness breathe through your body and let your heart go outwards to receive and give great joy. You will feel the heartbeat of others and it will draw you closer. Emmanuel is here. Emmanuel is a musician, his music is all round you. Listen. Be patient. Enrique and Josephina are others close to you. Let them talk to you. Mendelsohn may mean something to you. Think on and wait. I am happy that we have spoken again. Great strides will be made by you but I am tired now so we will speak again soon. Elephally"

So here were the famous names that Elephally had told me previously would be forthcoming. As before, I immediately went on the internet to look up Emmanuel, the musician. I found an Emmanuel Chabrier (1841-1894) and also, grouped as musicians with him, Clara Schumann (nee Clara Josephine Wieck, 1819-1896) and Enrique Granados (1867-1916)[9]. Mendelssohn lived from 1809-1847, so was of the same era. I had not known that Clara Schumann had the middle name 'Josephine'[10] and I had certainly never heard of Emmanuel Chabrier or Enrique Granados.

I was startled out of my reverie by the telephone. It was George calling to say that the wedding had gone well for him.

Was it a coincidence that he should ring at this moment? I told him that I knew he had enjoyed his wedding as I had just been writing about it and that I was to tell him that "Thomas is very happy". George, couldn't help himself; he burst into tears and said that I couldn't possibly know how much that meant to him and how happy it had made him. He said it was the best message he had ever received and that it meant an awful lot to him.

I had been reading a book entitled *The Serpent of Light: Beyond 2012* written by Drunvalo Melchizedek[11]. One of my fellow Circle members had lent it to me, as she knew we were planning a trip to South America in 2011. The book was having a profound impact on me. I read that "every 13,000 years on Earth, a sacred and secret event takes place that changes everything, an event that changes the very course of history. And at this moment, this rare event is occurring."

I read that this is all about the Earth's Kundalini and its energy. It is "attached to a single location on the surface of the Earth and stays there for a period of about 13,000 years. But then it moves to a new location for the next 13,000 years. And when it moves, our idea of what "spiritual" means changes. It transforms according to the new energies of the future cycle, leading us into a higher spiritual path."

I had nearly finished Melchizedek's book when I felt I should do some automatic writing, and what I wrote this time blew my mind. Undoubtedly I had been influenced by the book I was reading.

"Yes you must follow your thoughts. 2012 is your destiny and you will be thinking and doing more to help others through the transition. It will be a challenging time and you will help to guide those you believe in. There will be great winds and disasters but it will not destroy your planet. (There were indeed many natural disasters in 2012, including Hurricanes Sandy, Ernesto and Isaac (affecting the Caribbean, Mexico, USA and Canada); earthquakes in Iran, Afghanistan, the Philippines and China; flooding in North America and China; wildfires in the USA; tornadoes in Poland, Japan, Indonesia and Turkey; avalanches in

Afghanistan and Pakistan and cyclones in Sri Lanka and India). *It will cause your people to re-evaluate what they believe in and what they live for. It will be the end of greed and people will start to love and help one another. There will be more communication with other planets and people you have yet to meet. The world will become a very different place for you to live in. You will be guided by your heart and soul and your trust in God.*

You must find time to start studying and preparing yourself and others for what is to come. Visit Mexico and see the Mayan culture for there is much for you to learn. It is destined for you to do this. You are strong and will find the way forward. You will help many more people on their journey of understanding. Do not be afraid. Think positively when there is gloom for you will go past this onto a brighter and more fulfilling life, filled with light and happiness. Breathe through your heart and know that all will be well. This is your time to prepare.

Study the philosophers. Case and Blenmire to start. You are starting to understand your pathway. It is not what George has envisaged. This is much greater but you will do it without hesitation. Think of this as a great journey, as part of your travelling to understand a different way of life.

The sun will become very hot and scorch the earth but there will be hiding places which you must seek out in preparation. You will find this place on your travels and you will know and be in place when events occur. It will be cataclysmic but you and others will survive. Know that your life as you know it at the moment will change but you will not look back as you will have a greater understanding of life and how it is made.

Case, Case, Case, you read about him. You have been told about him before by others. It is no coincidence. I am not frightening you but you must be prepared. We will help and guide you. You will find the right people to talk to. You have not yet encountered them but they will find you. Keep the Circle close to you as they are there to support and there is much love there from the heart. These are your true friends. Keep them with you and entrust your thoughts as they will offer advice and guidance and in return you will help them. Remember the children for they are the innocents who need to be nurtured. Keep a cross with you at all times for this will protect you."

I assumed that the "Case" referred to was Edgar Cayce. Nowhere could I find the name of Benmire.

At the next Circle meeting I attended I read my last two writings to my friends. It sparked quite a debate, as one of the members said that there was a belief that 2012 was a year out and that changes would take place one year earlier in 2011 – when I was due to be in Mexico, the home of the ancient Mayan and Aztec civilisations.

The meditation that day was exactly the same as the first one I had been given by George, some two years earlier. It involved envisaging a pink mountain with a building at the top and going through a doorway. My meditation this time was extremely fragmented. I saw the mountain which was in the shape of a pink pyramid, as if it had a picture frame around it, and I also saw it through an "eye". I found myself in a market place, which felt as if it was inside the pyramid, and I took the hands of various children and led them forwards, past a smiling Nero (my Roman soldier guide). I then saw a white owl and then a tablet with letters on it.

George's translation of this: I was now seeing through my "third eye" and would be healing the world through wisdom. What was more important to me was the "eye" I had seen. Did this mean that I now would start to be able to see and feel more through my "third eye"?

To be honest I was again growing rather sceptical of the Circle meetings, wondering whether things weren't getting a little far-fetched. It was therefore some time before I attempted any further contact with Elephally. However, prompted by Mark, I once again sat down and put pen to paper:

"Listen to what you hear all around you. You are waiting for a big event in your life. You must prepare and be ready to receive the news that you will be given. You must listen more and meditate so that you can raise your vibrations to be in tune with us. You have

seen the third eye and you must start to focus more on this to see ahead of your time. Know that you will be walking towards the light but will be enveloped in a large mist swirling all around you. There will be high winds and the trees will lose their leaves. You will never have seen anything like this before. You will shield your eyes against the dust but all the time the light will filter through the fog and you will be guided along to the other side to be with the others who have also been shown the pathway to freedom of your spirit. There are many who are preparing for this moment when your world will change to a different level of understanding.

John Bright is a name you should look for. Astrologers think they know all there is to know but they are wrong. There is so much more for you to learn about your universe. Look for John Bright and others in his circle. He knows you are coming to find him and is waiting but you must first discover the way. This is a challenge we are setting you as when you have mastered this you will have the faith to continue with your work, which will then become very clear.

No, you will not be going on a long journey to find John Bright, he is close by, but you will have to venture to other countries in your preparation for the new world. You time is fast approaching and you will find a new motivation to learn and discover new talents which will help you and others to survive the high winds and storms that you will encounter as you climb out into the sun.

Victor George the Elder, Roseanna and Gaynor will be names that you will come to know. Little John is also close by to help you understand. Use the ability of your pen to write and inform. Messages will be sent to you to convey to others. But first you must find John Bright. Look to the light and know serenity and peacefulness. We are all around you, you can almost feel us gathering close for we are all watching and interested to see you work. Feel the warmth around you. Go now and make your discoveries. Bon voyage as you say. Elephally"

Again, none of the names mentioned meant anything to me. I looked on the internet and found that in the past there had been a John Bright (16 November 1811 – 27 March 1889), who was a famous Quaker, a British Radical and Liberal statesman[12].

He led the repeal for the abolition of the Corn Laws. He spoke out against slavery and campaigned for an extension of voting rights. He was also a personal friend of Disraeli and lived at the same time as Gladstone (mentioned before in my writings).

I was, however, not convinced that this was the John Bright I was trying to find.

CHAPTER 20

Finding my Pathway

Again, my husband prompted me to contact Elephally, and when I did so, there didn't really seem to be anything new:

"Hello again it has been a long time and I have much to tell you. You are going to go on a long journey into another world, one that you do not understand or know about. You must listen and look through your third eye. Let me guide you but you must listen to what your own self tells you to do. Mark knows too that the time is right and will go with you. Trust him as your valued help and support. Pack a suitcase with your memories as this will give you knowledge on your quest. You are going to listen and talk to many people. Do not be afraid for it is written in time that this is your purpose in life and you are well equipped to handle what is coming your way.

Remember the colour blue, yes this is a healing colour but it also means that you will cross water. Your house will sell and you will then be ready to venture to new places. You will find new friends who will understand what you are doing and help you. I keep telling you to stand by the trees and to wear a cross as this will protect you. I am sitting here beside you.

Go to bed and dream, for what you will see will be your pathway. You are still learning and need to have more confidence.

Listen with your heart and be open to others around you. Help those in need, those who do not understand what is happening to them. Be ready for change. Elephally loves you."

Well, this just seemed to be more of the same, although I did start to wear a cross.

A week later, sitting under a walnut tree having lunch at a friend's house, I was about to have the positive proof that I was looking for to take me out of my complacency and inertia.

We were playing around and Mark borrowed a pendant to use as a pendulum to show how he obtained a "yes" and a "no" to questions. Suitably impressed by Mark's abilities, I found myself first of all taking an elderly lady's watch and holding it in my hand. I saw an old gentleman with slicked back grey hair, wearing a blue suit, standing very erect and holding what looked like some sort of baton or walking stick. I was convinced that it was this lady's husband who had passed to the other side but had been in the RAF during his time on earth. The baton would have been his pace stick.

However, I then took the ring of another friend and told him that although I believed he had been brought up in a town, I saw him in the countryside by a bale of hay with a young friend. This drew a very short intake of breath from my friend, who indicated that he knew exactly what I was referring to. I then told him that I had had a vision earlier and it had come back to me again, of him straddling a motorway. This further shocked him and his partner, who both immediately knew what I was referring to, even if I didn't. In fact, it had such an impact on him that it reduced him to tears. George, who was also present at the lunch, told me that these would be tears of happiness and he was incredibly proud of what I had just done. I was shocked to my inner core that I had given my friend two such meaningful messages. This was my personal proof that all that I was striving for and wanting belief in existed.

The following day was another Circle meeting, and after sharing my recent writings with George, he suggested that John Bright was on the other side and that I should make contact with Elephally again to ask him questions. So when I returned home, this is what I wrote:

"Hello Elephally, it's me and I am going to start writing to you as I have many questions and would like to know if John Bright is this side or has passed to your side and also is Little John my Circle leader?"

Elephally's reply:

"You are being very inquisitive. John Bright is this side, he is in spirit. He will be helping to guide you but you still have much more to discover and, yes, you know Little John.

John (Bright) is asking me to tell you that you are very clever to find him so quickly and that you must continue to find out and learn more about him. You must look to see where he was born as you will discover that you know this area, although you are no longer living here.

Eliza is a name that you will find. The teachings of George are becoming more relevant to your work, as you learn to interpret and understand all around you. Do not be surprised that you will start to see and hear more. Listen to the gentleman you will meet on Monday at your Circle meeting. He will have a message for you. He does not know this yet but when he meets you, he will understand what he must say and you too will have messages for him as there will be a link between the two of you.

Pitter patter as you hear the sound of feet along the cobble stones. It is not the sound of human's feet — it is a donkey finding his way to you to help you carry your burden of life. He has sturdy feet and baskets for your understanding. Let him help you take the strain. You will be meeting other Circle members as you journey in your understanding. Keep writing and listening for the voices that you will hear and the bells that will ring out.

You have known Little John before in your previous life times on earth. Your previous lives have not been easy ones. I am happy that you have discovered your place in the mountains and that there is rebirth there now. You will find evidence of other lives you have led on your earthly planet. There is an old man walking along the beach towards you with his hands outstretched. It is getting dark and the sun is setting but he is very happy to see you. Yes it is an Indian gentleman with a white shawl around him and very skinny bonny legs. This is your Little John and you are meeting again. He was a very wise old guru and his spirit lives on. He too will start to remember more as your journey becomes clearer. Ask him about the windmills. You will be surprised"

Going quickly onto the internet I was flabbergasted to discover that John Bright's wife was called Elizabeth[13] (Eliza) and that she died in 1841 in Leamington – a town in the UK, close to where I was brought up as a child.

So I had known George in a previous life, except he was then known as Little John. When I asked George about "windmills" all he could say was that windmills, as a symbol, meant a friendly place and signified happy times.

CHAPTER 21

My Destiny

At our next Circle meeting, George introduced a friend of his (was this the gentleman Elephally had referred to in his last message?), who had also been part of George's original Circle. This friend was present for us to pass messages to. This was to prove another turning point for me, as I found that whilst holding a set of his keys, I was able to give him an accurate reading of events that had happened in his life. I was able to give him names of people and animals known to him who had passed to the other side. These were the messages that Elephally had predicted I would give this person.

In turn, I was told that my writings would prove to be teachings for me and that I would join another Circle in approximately two years' time in order to be able to progress further. George told me that he too knew this and also that Elephally had told him what my destiny is to be! Unfortunately he didn't pass that knowledge on to me!!

After this meeting I didn't feel the need to contact Elephally again until a couple of weeks' later when I received the following message:

"Clairvoyance is a gift being given to you so that you can tell others our messages and help them to believe. It takes time to learn

these skills as others have done before you. Edgar Case as you know is one such person who had many gifts and you will be the same. You need to have patience and be willing to learn and not be afraid of what others will think of you. Eileen is another name for you. This is your aunt on spirit side and she wants to tell you that she now understands why you have been chosen to follow this pathway. She says her daughter too is gifted in this way. Brian look after him for he is going to need more surgery for his heart (This happened). *You must start giving people messages from your heart. Do not let their tears upset you for what you are doing is good for them.*

Mark has been very clever to find Atlantis and you must learn more about this civilisation as it will help when your world changes again. There are many lessons to be learnt. It is the right time for your world to discover what happened to Atlantis. You were correct a long time ago when you went to the Canary Islands, for you have lived here before in the City of Atlantis. You will remember more and use this information.

Peter Piper, John Rapier are names for you. You are getting quite a collection which will show you a link that has much meaning. Remember this is your pathway of discovery that will take you into a new world of wisdom and colour and insight. George Bluewater. Think on. What does this name mean to you? You have a gift of playing the piano. You have played music before in your previous lives. Here is another link for you. Your hands have always been important as a doctor, as a pianist and as a writer. Use your skills to help others again. You and Little John are both gurus. It is the same as what you are doing now. Let yourself relax so that you can remember how you passed wisdom on to others. There is much in the message for you to think about. Take your time and we look forward to seeing you progress further. You are doing well and you are happy as we are for you as our child. Elephally is proud. Go now and learn. Elephally."

Well, none of the names this time meant anything to me, nor could I find anything on the internet that had any meaning. So time will tell. I shall have to wait for this message to become clearer.

A few Circle meetings later, another turning point was reached, and this particular meeting stretched us all. We were asked to tell the person on the right of us who the guide was sitting beside them. I was told that I had a Samurai warrior beside me, who is my door keeper and protector. George told me that this meant I had nothing to fear, as this warrior would always look after me. He said it was highly likely that I would start to go "off with the fairies", or put more simply go into a trance, and that with the Samurai warrior beside me, I had nothing to fear. He said that I might even find that whilst doing my automatic writing I would find that I would go into a trance and come to, to find that I had written much without being aware of writing! He also said that my writing would take a different turn in its messages.

Another interesting thing happened when I told the person on my right who her guide was. I had a number of names all crowding into my mind. Firstly, Gladys, then Victoria, then Penelope, and I decided to go with Penelope and told Sarah that she had worked with his person. Sarah told me that she couldn't take the name Penelope but she certainly could take a Gladys. George told me that this was a lesson; that I should always take the first contact given, as many other spirits try to push their way in to also make contact.

The vibrations in our Circle meetings had also altered. Mark had changed and was bringing in a much more light-hearted and humorous contribution.

At the end of the meeting, George asked us all to think about the type of medium we all thought we were destined to be.

I feel ready now to take more giant steps forward, with the lessons I have learned.

Well, our Circle meetings continued very much along the same vein, with each of us passing clairvoyant messages to other Circle members. George was suggesting to us that we go to a nearby town to a gathering of people, to give them messages. None of us really felt comfortable with this. I didn't really feel much of a need to contact Elephally for another month either, when I received the following message:

"You are trying too hard and must be patient. Your Circle is progressing in the way it should and you are all getting more confident in your ability to help others. However you must be careful in those that you trust for not all people will take you seriously and this will cause difficulties for you. Take your time with one or two trusted helpers who we will send to you. You will know who these people are. They will not be "star gazers". There are many around you who think in the same way and are interested in your work. Choose with care who you trust for you do not want your work ridiculed.

There is a young girl with golden hair who is trying to contact you and who needs your help. She will become known to you soon and you will need to give her care and love and support.

You are entering a new phase of your work and your clairvoyance is developing so that you will be able to pass on messages to others but you must practice so that you are certain about the messages you are giving. You need to know that these are true and real to those around you waiting for your help. It will help those who have lost loved ones and will give them strength to continue in their lives. Use your third eye which you are starting to use. Look through this eye at the world beyond yours. Look high into the sky.

You must start looking at the auras of others as this will tell you much about these people as to whether they are good or bad. This is what I am talking about when you give your readings. Trust yourself and you will do no wrong.

George Hamilton is a name for you. Your guides are close to you and they want you to feel this man's vibrations. Think about this name and what it means.

Wonders of the world and what it takes. They did not understand that my little bird was only trying to heal me and they acted out of ignorance at your work. You have been a clairvoyant before and you are regaining your powers but years of oppression have left their mark. You will remember the ducking stool and the tight band around your mouth, so that you couldn't speak and you are now fighting these memories so that you can again help others. You had a white hat with flaps down the side of your face and a blue dress tight at the waist and ballooning down to your feet. Learn from your past. You will still find those who doubt you and do not believe. You must overcome this to follow your pathway. Many things will happen in your world which will be new to you and those around you. Remember you will be protected. Yes there is a name of Mary, the mother of Jesus. She is the mother of you all and will give you comfort in the years ahead that you face. You must talk to her for she will give you help and succour. You will find what you are looking for. Have faith. Focus on colours."

I also looked on the internet and found Sir George Hamilton, 1st Baronet of Danalong (1607-1679) who was married to Mary Butler [14]. Was this what Elephally had meant when he said "think about this name and what it means"?

Anyway, Elephally's message cleared any doubt in my mind that I had made the right decision not to visit the gathering in our nearby town, which George had suggested. I did feel that not everyone I talked to would understand the path I had chosen to follow and my new beliefs.

Instead, we agreed that George should arrange for another two people to visit our Circle so that we could pass messages on to them. We all felt that if these people made the effort to visit us, then they were more likely to be in genuine need of our help rather than an afternoon's entertainment.

Just before the Circle meeting where we were due to meet our two volunteers, I again contacted Elephally:

"You are not alone. We are here and listening. We have many messages for you which we are waiting to give. You must listen carefully and relate them exactly as you hear them. One of the people today is quite distressed and you must emphasise and be clear in what you say so that you do not cause additional stress.

Your pathway is becoming clearer to you and you are becoming more focused. You are also becoming more open. The skies are clear and you will see the bright light beaming down towards you as we connect our minds together. Look towards the light as this will open our channel to you. Do not take on the problems of others, act only as a conduit to help them understand what they have to do and think.

Many things will become clearer to you. Do not try too hard. You must relax so that we can tune into your vibrations. All of you are doing well and we are very pleased with your progress. You will be delighted, as we will be, with what you achieve this afternoon. Be prepared for surprises. You will have to be patient and we will talk soon. Elephally."

As soon as we opened the Circle that afternoon, we were all ready to pass on our messages, which came thick and fast. At the start I heard the word "guns", which I saw shooting towards birds in the sky, and I also saw a small white and brown spaniel dog. I interpreted this to mean that the gun was about to start changes in the first lady´s life; that she was about to free her life of troubles and that she would move forward in the knowledge that she had faithful friends around her helping her along. At this the lady burst into tears of happiness and accepted the message.

I also saw a birthday cake for the second lady, signifying an anniversary of a passing. Then I also saw a beige straw hat with the brim turned upwards. Lady No 2 took the message saying that it would shortly be the anniversary of the passing of her mother and that her mother used to wear such a hat.

Jessica became extremely tearful when she said that she felt the presence of a child on the other side who she felt was very close to Lady No 2 and that there was a lot of love for this lady. Lady No 2 confirmed that she had lost her child, when she was two years old.

At one point I held the watch of Lady No 1 and saw her standing in a field with sheep beside her. I also saw water and strongly felt that she would be moving to a colder climate where she would need woolly jumpers. I felt that this was the move that she had been considering and I strongly felt that this would be the right move for her and that she had the support of many good friends, albeit she kept these friends at a distance. I felt that she should allow herself to become closer to these friends and accept their help. Again Lady No 1 was in tears and confirmed all that I had said to her.

These are only a few examples of the messages we passed on that afternoon. All the messages were accurate and continually produced tears of happiness for the two ladies. Some of us were crying too with the emotion of the messages being passed across. I couldn't help reflecting on just how far we had all progressed since the start of the Circle meetings, in our journey to understanding clairvoyance and in all our abilities to pass on meaningful messages.

George later called me to let me know that Lady No 1 had left that afternoon with a smile on her face and that she had now made up her mind to go back to the UK to start living her life again after the death of her husband. No wonder that Elephally had said that one of the ladies was distressed. We had all been responsible for starting her road to recovery. All our messages, George said, had been spiritual ones that had greatly benefited both ladies, Lady No 2 having also been totally thrilled with the messages she had received.

Again there was a long gap between my attendance at Circle meetings. Just before I attended again I received the following message from Elephally:

"Not long ago you were unhappy about yourself. Now you have reason to be very happy for you are advancing well. You are learning your lessons and are applying what you are learning. It does not matter that we do not speak often as I know that you have me in your thoughts and actions to help others. There are many more people who will need your help. So you must continue to concentrate and listen to the voice of help. Do not rush. You will hear when you are needed.

Listen to the silence for it is not silence that you hear. You hear the wind around you and you feel us and our presence in that wind. Never fear that you are alone, for we will always be with you. You will shortly be entering a new phase of your development and you will be taken by surprise with what you achieve. Do not try too hard for it will all come easily for you and the rest of your "Circle".

You are all very close and have a good understanding of each other and you work well together. It will soon be time for you all to help others. Sarah will be returning to you. She is learning many lessons about herself and her ability to help others. Your furry friends too have an empathy with your tasks. They are intuitive to the needs of humans even though they cannot speak to you they seek to offer support and friendship and love to help you on your pathways.

You must stop looking for spectacular messages now, for you are past this. You must now concentrate on yourself and your development as we are close and watching and helping. Trust in yourself. Elephally."

At the Circle meeting George opened by saying that the spirits had decided that the time was now right for us to understand what happens when we pass over to the other side, and that we would be entering a new phase: pretty much what Elephally had told me. During the meeting we continued to pass messages to each other which were meaningful, but nothing mind-blowing.

However, at the following Circle meeting, when I got up to pass on a message from my guide, I saw the head of white horse but was unable to see who was sitting on this horse. I could only focus on this horse's eye, and I translate this vision to mean strength and light. As I waited for a message, I was conscious of being taken out of myself, almost as if the spirits were about to take me over, but I think I was concentrating too hard and after a few minutes the feeling passed.

Not long after, I received the following message from Elephally:

"High on a hill there is a music box for you. Listen and you will hear it. Be patient and keep looking at all the things around you. For you will see and hear and feel all that we will be giving you on your journey into the unknown.

Jim is a name that will be important. Jim Whitehead wants to be remembered to Jessica. There are many of us waiting to be able to connect with you. Look at the box for it will open for you and you will see many stars and bright lights in the arena. There are also horses around you. Beautiful grey stallions that can race with the wind. Your mind is being divided and you need to concentrate on the side that you choose to follow for it will become very clear to you shortly what you must do to carry yourself forward. Remember your past and seek to find the answers that you are looking for.

Your pathway is clear and is easy to follow but you must concentrate and meditate for this is how we will communicate with you all. You cannot just wait for things to happen you must prompt and make things happen and you will understand much more through communication in meditation. Each day you will set aside a time and place so that we can prepare ourselves for your lessons. There is a lot to teach you in a short space of time. Remember all is light and happiness.

Look at the music sheets and remember the names I have given you.

George Osborne. Watch this man for he has the power to lead and be successful in his path that he has chosen. Watch the children as they grow and watch how they learn. Keep looking at the box for it will open with many surprises for you all. Tell Mark he will see more and more. Tell him to feel the hand on his shoulder and he will feel the direction in which he is being turned. Peter too must continue to look at the cards. Jenny must look up and feel lighter, she will hear and understand. Ask her about Roger. We are looking after Anne and she will be returning to you after her period of recovery.

Go now and give these messages and the others that we will pass to you this afternoon. There is a wall which is significant to you. Remember this. Elephally."

CHAPTER 22

Elephally's Plans for Me

"In the end you will make news and events will guide you along your pathway. You have been silent but now you must start to speak to others and find the way ahead for all. You will be encouraged by what you hear and think. Every where around you there are people who need help. You need to feel their pain to help them recover. From the beginning of time there have been those who have been able to hear and feel and help. You are not a stranger to helping others but you have forgotten your ability and powers and now you must start to remember all that you have learned in your previous lives.

You have been sleeping and now you must awaken for the time is coming closer to the time you will be needed. Do not be afraid for we are with you and guiding you. You have not always been a good person but you have learned that your wrongs need to be righted and you are now at peace with yourself and your soul.

There are many pathways for you to choose but you will know the right one for you. Listen, listen to the silence and the winds of change. Look at the colours of the sun on green leaves, at the red of the sunset and also at the greys and colours in between. This is a good place for you as you are discovering. This will be your journeys end as you will find meaning here. You can make yourself understood. Look below the surface and see the suffering of past *souls lost here. You already know how to help them. Concentrate on the sunsets and the light and be aware of those close to you seeking their own way forward. Help them to go to the light. Sit in quiet contemplation and meditate so that we can speak to you further in your mind. Your guides are close by and want to talk to you. They have been waiting for the right time and now is the right time. Listen, watch, hear and feel. Go with the wind. Elephally."*

I felt that after this blessing from Elephally that I was nearing the end of my participation in the Circle. At the same time, it was becoming more and more difficult for us to attend Circle meetings, and when Jessica and Peter decided that the time had come to withdraw, Mark and I too felt we had come to the point when we too should stop attending meetings; that we could now continue on our pathways independently, benefiting from the guidance that we had received from George and Anne at our weekly Circle meetings.

Our decision to withdraw elicited the following message from Elephally:

"I am always there for you whenever you need to feel the guidance and enlightenment. You must not worry or be concerned if you do not continue to go to the Circle meetings. These meetings are to help you focus and concentrate on a regular basis but there is nothing to stop you doing this by yourself. Mark will find his own way and he too will continue to see the light. All will not be lost as you have learned many lessons which you will not forget in time.

I will always be with you, guiding you along your pathway. Do not be afraid for your pathway was determined a long time ago. Go with the light, keep in contact by meditating. You will not lose your way. Messages will still be passed to you so that you can help others. You have learned much and are a better person for your perseverance. Tell George not to fret for he has done a good job in guiding you all but it is now time for George to take a rest and focus on himself and his family. The time is right for your decisions and he will know this.

You will always be good friends and he will still be there to guide you. George now needs to concentrate on himself and his needs and care. Go now with the light and happiness that you will have all your days on the earth plane. There is still much work for you to do and this will become clear to you. Focus and keep an open mind and all will be revealed. Your time is now. Enjoy all that will be happening to you and Mark, for you will be sharing this journey together in your life together. Go with grace and good will. Yours for ever Elephally."

And so we had Elephally's blessing to continue …

CHAPTER 23

Waiting for Elephally's Sign

Well, I wasn't particularly good at keeping my word, or maybe the time wasn't quite right. I did think about Elephally and talked to him, but I didn't feel inspired to try my automatic writing again for another two months.

"We are in contact again after a long time! You are not alone in your life and you must recognise this. Time is passing by and you must act and keep going for there is much to do. I cannot talk about what this is, you must find out for yourself. This is a very busy time for all of us. My friends and yours are all here looking and watching you. There will be a sign that will be sent to you, you must watch out for this as the time is near. You will know when you receive the sign and you will know how to act. You have been prepared for your journey into time.

Mark is finding out more and more daily about your lives and ours and how we have lived and helped others in the past. Do not be afraid with what you will see, for the people you will see will be friendly and helpful. There will be a bright light and you will see images that are strange and unknown to you, but this is our presence that will be visiting you. Around the time of the second moon. Prepare yourself for a different life and one where you will be helping others. It will be an enormous step forward for you but you are capable of this now and will understand all that you have been taught and heard.

Keep listening for my messages for the time is coming closer for you. Do not be afraid for I will be there to guide you. Your life will change, but it will be for the better. Go now in peace. Elephally".

Amazingly, another year passed before I contacted Elephally again:

"Don't push yourself so hard, you have plenty of time and you are still learning about yourself and how to fit into our world. Life is not simple and cannot be learned easily or quickly. Put yourself into a relaxed position and close your eyes and let yourself relax and be open. You will feel lightness and need to look beyond your sight. Feel yourself relax and close out all obstructions. We are waiting and you will recognise all your guides. Be open and listen to what they have to say to you.

Follow the mountain pathway upwards over the stones. Doctor will call you for help in understanding. Not you, you are safe and secure. Others need your help as you will become a doctor in mind and spirit, not a medical doctor but one who understands the mind and actions that have been set many centuries in many life times. Listen, keep listening and you will hear. It is good that you heard me today and that we speak to each other. Be open and listen. Elephally."

Again, at Mark's prompting, I contacted Elephally again whilst we were holidaying in Mexico, visiting the sacred site of Teotihuacan. The Aztecs believed that the gods created the universe in this ancient city that once flourished as the epicentre of culture and commerce. The name of the site, literally, means "place of the gods".

Elephally´s words to me were:

"It has been a long time but it is not long at all for me and you. Time for me no longer has no meaning, it is only on your earth plane where you measure time. You must take your time to find meaning for you and for you to understand your life and what its meaning is. You have contact all around you. You are close to your earth's core and will feel the heat and warmth being given to you for events and timings will become clearer to you. You are seeing

much happening in the world around you. More will happen soon. Do not be disheartened for all your training with George is not lost and you will come to see our teachings as a great gift.

Muse on and think about what is happening to those closest to you, as there are lessons to be learned here and you with all new wisdom and insight will be able to do much to help. You will hear the call of others for your wisdom and guidance for we will be passing messages to them through you. Many people are not able to see what is obvious and the course they should take. Be there to guide them.

Lean on the big elephant, absorb his strength and fight on. You are small but you are strong in heart and mind and soul. You will hear, we will contact you when we need you. It is good that you keep in contact.

Grains of sand will filter through your fingers but you will know what to keep, you will know what is important. Look for the stones to keep close for your protection. Listen, keep listening and you will hear. Do not give up on your search for the truth. I am going now as I have many others to see and help as you will too in time. Yours elephally".

Since Mark and I stopped going to the Circle, neither of us at any stage forgot what we had learned and experienced. In fact, ironically, we became more confident in talking to others about our experiences and, where appropriate, we would do readings for friends, which always, amazingly, were pretty accurate. I also on one occasion read out to friends some of the writings that Elephally had given me. Apparently my whole facial expression changed when I did this.

I'm still waiting to find out where all this is leading. Time, I guess, will reveal all.

CHAPTER 24

Realisation

Again, another year had passed since I had written my last entry into this book and I had long wondered how it would end. When would I receive the promised sign from Elephally? More to the point, how would I know how to act when I received the sign? Then suddenly, in a flash, it came to me and was the reason for writing this book.

On Christmas Day 2015 my beloved father collapsed and was rushed into hospital. Shortly thereafter he was diagnosed with terminal lung cancer. We had many long conversations together about what he was facing, and then there was the question: "Are you religious – do you think there is something there after we die?" My answer was that I was not particularly religious but I did emphatically believe in life after death. Was this the sign that Elephally had promised?

I knew then what the purpose of this book was, and that this was the sign I had been waiting for. I understood why I had been invited to join the Circle, and why I had been receiving messages from Elephally. I understood that all the messages and teachings I had been receiving were to be used to help others by publishing my experiences written in this book. My mother told me that as my father slipped away from this life he opened his eyes one last time to say goodbye. His lovely blue eyes were radiating a wonderful bright light, letting her know that he had found the light.

I had received Elephally's sign, and I knew now how to act. It was to help my father and those like him to understand what they are about to encounter; to know that there is life after death, and for them to feel the love and kindness they will receive when they pass on.

That, put simply, was my purpose in life, as guided by Elephally. It was to speak to others and to help prepare those who are dying for what they are about to encounter when they pass away to the other side, and to guide them to find the light, thus ensuring a smooth and peaceful transition to the other side, where all their family and friends would be waiting for them. To let everyone know that there is nothing to fear from the unknown, and that they should look forward to another big and happy adventure in the hereafter. To offer comfort to their loved ones, who are left behind on this earth, by giving them the understanding that none of us really die and that there is existence beyond the grave, where we are cared for with love and kindness.

After all, I am living testimony to the fact that I have lived a life before my existing one. I had been given the proof of where I lived and who my family were. I had also been given provable evidence from my spirit guide, Elephally, not only of his previous existence on earth in Libya (that could be tracked with the facts he gave me) but also of the existence of other peoples' relationships in the past (Tennyson and Disraeli, John Bright, the Quaker, and his wife Elizabeth), details of which I could not possibly have known about. I knew that, as with the souls in Thailand left after the tsunami, not knowing how to find the light to the other side, and my journey to Thailand to help them find it, that this was what I had been preparing for – to help others to find the light. To help others understand. By writing about my experiences, I knew that I could help others. This was Elephally's goal, and now mine.

I sincerely hope that the experiences I have written about in this book, which have so enlightened me in my belief in life after death, will help all those, when their time comes, to have closure in this life and find their way to the next one, in the strong belief that not all ends here and that they have much to look forward to.

Many of Elephally's words have been symbolic, and need to be interpreted in a wider sense. I hope that I have been able to interpret them so that readers of this book will find them meaningful. To the best of my ability I have tried to interpret them in the best way to help others.

My journey is still continuing. I have much more work left to do. I have yet to visit Libya and, as Elephally, my patient and caring guide has told me, I have many more things still to do on the earth plane to help people.

I look forward to all the new experiences and learnings that will be coming my way and to sharing these with you.

Astraken

Astraken

REFERENCES/ENDNOTES

Chapter 1: My First Circle Meeting
1   Shirley MacLaine Out on a Limb. Bantam Books. Published 1983
2   Morris West The Clowns of God. Coronet Books. Published 1981
3   John G Fuller The Ghost of Flight 401. Berkley Publishing Corporation, Distributed by G.P. Putman´s Sohns. First published 1 June 1976

Chapter 8: Experiencing Automatic Writing
4   Matthew Manning
     https://en.wikipedia.org/wiki/Matthew_Manning
5   Neale Donald Walsh Conversations with God.
     https://en.wikipedia.org/wiki/Conversations_with_God

Chapter 12: Previous Lives
6   Map of Libya. ITMB Publishing - International Travel Maps Libya
7   Photographs of the Awbari Lakes, Libya.
     https://www.temehu.com/Cities_sites/Gabroun.htm

Chapter 19: Proof and Prophecies from Elephally
8   https://en.wikipedia.org/wiki/Alfred,_Lord_Tennyson
9   The Piano Quarterly – Volume 39 – Page 32. Piano Incorporated 1990.
     https://books.google.es/books?id=qooJAQAAMAAJ&q=Emmanuel+Chabrier,+Clara+Schumann,+Enrique+Granados&dq=Emmanuel+Chabrier,+Clara+Schumann,+Enrique+Granados&hl=en&sa=X&ved=0ahUKEwimqI-I58fWAhWMWxQKHaqrDocQ6AEILDAB

10 https://en.wikipedia.org/wiki/Clara_Schumann

11 Drunvalo Melchizadek, The Serpent of Light: Beyond
    2012 – The Movement of the Earths Kundalini and the
    Rise of the Female Light 1949-2013. Weiser Books.
    Published 2008

12 https//www.en.wikipedia.org/wiki/John_Bright

Chapter 20: Finding my Pathway

13 https//www.ancestry.com(genealogy/records/elizabeth-
    priestman-23306641

Chapter 21: My Destiny

14 https//en.wikipedia.org/wiki/Sir_Geroge_
    Hamilton,_1st_Baronet,_of-Donalong

Astroken

Astroken

Astroken

Lightning Source UK Ltd.
Milton Keynes UK
UKHW04f0734170818
327398UK00001B/120/P